Surthriving Special Education

Education

The Special Educator's Best Friend

Lisle MED

Table of Contents

Preface

Special education is a very misunderstood profession. It isn't teaching, per se. It isn't nursing, per se. It isn't psychology, per se. It isn't social work, per se. Yet, special education is all of these things and any professional who is inspired to do the work or even deigns to do so out of seeking job security and smaller class sizes needs to understand that special education is more than it appears. To do it right, to do it consistently, to do it for the benefit of students with disabilities requires a level of dedication, knowledge, and professionalism that may not be present in your school building. The landscape of K-12 education in the United States isn't the beacon of hope and humility that it was in decades past (which was first made apparent as early as the 70s if we're all honest). Schools are increasingly overcrowded, there is a glaring teacher shortage, unless you live around a major city you may not be getting paid very well for your work, and all of this does not logically suggest that those left in the classroom and in leadership are the "best candidates" as we say in the job market. Still, there are great schools left, there are great students to teach, there are great communities to become a part of, and there is great work do. This is of particular significance to the special educator because special educators sit in a particularly unique space within schools. They are serving students that are historically at the bottom of the academic curve, students who have some of the most difficult social circumstances, and who are the most likely to have behavior or disciplinary issues in the classroom. A special educator has the ability to change the entire narrative of a school just by doing their job well. It doesn't have to require any special funding, field trips, PBIS grants, or even an exciting STEM program. All it takes is one special educator knowing what they're doing and doing it when it's required. On one hand, special education takes a lot of work, but on the other it can be easy and even fun. So, how do you keep special educators in the classroom to do this work when so many teaching professionals are leaving? To keep you in the classroom, to keep you with your students, to make you aware and knowledgeable, to give you the tools you need to be successful, to make sure you thrive, this book is your survival guide.

Chapter 1: What is Special Education?

The first thing that any special educator needs to know about special education, before we get into what practices and knowledge is involved in being a great special educator, we have to talk about what special education even is. As you've read in the preface, special education isn't one thing or another on a conceptual level, it is an amalgamation of many different practices and professions that when done appropriately are greater than the sum of their parts. Moreover, the reason that it is still very necessary to define special education is because if you don't have a proper definition of special education, even in the case that having a multiplicity of definitions for special education is necessary to have a full scope of the work, you won't be able to do the work effectively. If you go into the work thinking that special education is just teaching in smaller groups, you won't do it effectively. If you go into the work thinking that special education is just giving students accommodations for things they can't do on their own, you won't do it effectively. If you go into the work thinking that special education is just documenting everything that the student produces for compliance purposes, you won't do it effectively. The reason why you'll fail is because special education is guided fundamentally by the Individualized Education Program, or IEP, and all programs have objectives. If you go into special education with the wrong objectives, you will not get the right results. In this first chapter of your survival guide we will be discussing the most useful definitions of special education.

The first definition that you need to understand to appropriately contextualize special education is this:

Special education is a range of services provided to students with disabilities in order for them to gain access to the general education curriculum.

This definition will likely differ slightly from other definitions that you may come across in special education. In fact, it differs from the definition of special education provided by the Individuals with Disabilities Education Act, or IDEA; the legislation that guides and assures that students with disabilities are entitled to and provided special education (which we will touch upon later). Yet, the reason why this definition is the first provided in this chapter is because it encapsulates some key components of special education that other definitions neglect.

A Range of Services

Special education is a range of services. This point is integral to any definition of special education because teaching isn't the only service provided to students with disabilities. Every special education student doesn't even receive teaching services. Special education includes a vast array of supplemental and related services that might include (but are not limited to) occupational therapy, counseling, physical therapy, speech therapy, and even consultative services which in some cases means the student is not even receiving instruction from a special educator. As a special educator it is your role to determine if any of these services are necessary or useful to a student with disabilities so that it can be provided to them in their IEP.

A range of service also implies a couple of things about special education. Firstly, it implies that there is a requirement or some level of compliance that is related to or due to the service's receiver. If an IEP team, the group of individuals that comes together to determine the content of the IEP, publishes any type of service in an IEP, that student is legally due those services without question. It is also to be implied that if those services are not rendered to that student, the student will not make improvements in those areas. If any educator goes into a classroom with a student with a disability, they need to understand that the student doesn't just need their accommodations or their services, they are due those services. IEPs are legal documents. The same way that students in the United States are legally required to be in school to receive their compulsory education (until about the age of 16 depending on your state), schools and teachers are legally required to provide the services identified by a student with a disability's IEP.

It also implies that special education isn't just teaching. As mentioned above there are a number of different services that a student with special needs can benefit from in their IEP including various forms of therapy. However, this also applies to teaching. Teaching as provided through an IEP is specially designed instruction. This segways into our second definition of Special Education provided by the IDEA.

"Special Education means specially designed instruction, at no cost to parents, to meet the unique needs of a child with a disability…"

Specially designed instruction essentially means that the type of instruction provided to the students is catered to their individual needs. This means that the instruction that they are provided can be limited to that which is provided by a general education teacher with only accommodation integration support provided by the IEP. It can also mean that the student is receiving a specific learning program in a special education setting that is designed to meet his/her needs. It also means that the special education service provider can have the authority through the IEP to provide any type of unique or novel teaching convention to the student to meet their educational needs which might mean things like student center inquiry, experiential learning, gamification, or play based learning. Instruction in a special education classroom may not necessarily or ever look like the instruction taking place in a general education setting. The teaching or instruction provided to students with IEPs should be a direct response to the needs of that student as outlined in their IEP.

Students with Disabilities

Now the second part of that initial definition includes the phrase "students with disabilities". The reason why this phrase is so important to our definition of special education is because a student cannot qualify for special education services unless they have been identified as a student with a disability. There is a very long evaluation process that takes place before a student is placed in special education and then periodically as the student matriculates to determine if that student continues to qualify for services under special education. One of those qualifications is that the student must have a disability as described by a number of programs or categories, one of them being specific learning disability. (We will review more about what a specific learning disability means later on in this survival guide) Essentially this evaluation is conducted by a licensed psychologist and supported by members of the school faculty and agreed upon by the IEP team.

Gain access to the general education curriculum

The last part of our definition is about the general purpose or objective of special education, and there are a lot of ways that you could look at this particular aspect of our definition. Special education, on a fundamental level, is provided so that students can meet the requirements of their K-12 education. In the case a student's disabilities are providing a barrier to their success at completing these requirements, they in turn would be eligible for special education services. On a more conceptual level, the purpose of K-12 education itself is to create effective citizens for our country; these are people who are well adjusted, can contribute to their communities, and can pursue happy and free lives. If a student with a disability cannot access the curriculum they cannot achieve said purpose. Statistically, it remains true that students with disabilities are more likely to be incarcerated, homeless, jobless, as well as subject to other negative life outcomes which are a burden on society (not to mention devastating to individuals, families, and communities). So, on a social level it is very important that persons with disabilities receive special education in schools.

Furthermore, this also implies that if a person with a disability has access to the curriculum, they won't necessarily require special education services. There is a plethora of exceptionalities through which a student might qualify for special education services. However, this is dependent upon the extent to which that exceptionality prevents a student from accessing the curriculum. There are students on the autism spectrum in and outside of special education. There are students with physical limitations in and outside of special education. Considering the ubiquity of this diagnosis, there are many students with attention deficit hyperactivity disorder in and outside of special education. Special education services are designed to help students access the curriculum, so it is the responsibilities of families and schools to determine (1) if a student should be evaluated for services and (2) after that evaluation whether that student qualifies for services, or if the student's needs can be met with regular teaching best practices. The value and importance of this discussion on determination and whether a student has a disability, or should qualify for services, and to what extent their disability impacts their learning is highly related to the concept of disproportionality in which certain minority and language diverse populations are overrepresented in special education.

Above we have unpacked a few definitions of special education that are most useful in the daily practice of special education. Now, we're going to review a few more abstract definitions or understandings that are necessary to appropriately contextualize the meaning and purpose of this work.

The Historical

In this definition we have to take a step back from the school and talk about the historical context of people with disabilities. Ultimately, people with disabilities are who special educators serve and a historical definition of the work of special education really speaks to the urgency of the work and the need for effective service. The key legislation for special education passed in 2004 was IDEA. This brought some monumental changes to the field of even working with people with disabilities let alone in school settings. However, prior to then and throughout the 1900s people with disabilities were subject to some of the most gruesome and inequitable treatment in human history. If we speak first to the higher functioning end of the spectrum of disability, people with very common exceptionalities were often very casually exited from places of learning. Colloquially it is very common to hear of grandparents and great-grandparents of today and yesteryear that they never finished high school or even 8th grade. This is because, socially, during much of the 20th century it was fairly easy to excuse young people from the responsibilities of their education to pursue more practical uses of their time (particularly if they were already literate) like work in cases of familial need or community culture. This is exacerbated for people with rather inconspicuous disabilities like dyslexia or an attention disorder who would likely not receive the individualized support they would have needed in classrooms and schools that were highly generalized for a narrow definition of instruction. The pervading logic of the time being closer to assessing whether a student is fit for education rather than education fit for the student. So, these students would voluntarily or involuntarily be excluded from educational institutions.

For more mild, moderate, and even severe and profound forms of disability, be it deafness to a traumatic brain injury that causes significant cognitive limitations, there were very few institutions that would accommodate the learning needs of people with these exceptionalities. Furthermore, as the arch of disability leans more toward the severe and profound end of that spectrum there is increasingly limited general understanding of the nature of disability. Hellen Keller, born in 1880, who had no cognitive disability, but was rather blind and deaf is a very famous example of one who was treated very much as if she was as close to animal as she was man prior to receiving the instruction Anne Sulivan an alumna of the Perkins School for the Blind. Hellen Keller later became an author and advocate for the rights of people with disabilities.

Despite Keller's achievements, it is worth noting that she was also someone who came from an elite family. For the overwhelmingly greater proportion of less fortunate people with these more overt forms of disability they were subject to confinement, homelessness, incarceration, abuse, and also commitment to various psychiatric asylums. These asylums were notorious for various forms of abuse like forced sterilization, lobotomization, neglect, malnourishment, and even medical experimentation.

The gruesome history of the treatment of people with disabilities isn't important to your definition of special education to be extremist or even alarmist about the things that you may witness or experience in a school setting, but it is to say that there is a natural archaic behavior that humans exhibit toward people who are different than them. This is true for people of different races. This is true of people of different languages. This is true of people of different ability. On a micro-level within schools today, some of these abuses still exist and lesser forms of these abuses are quite common. Special educators that resort to daily yelling and screaming at students with disabilities rather than the disciplined strategies that you'll be exposed to in this survival guide, general educators that throw up their hands and say they can't teach certain students because it's too hard and place them in the back of classrooms, school officials that resort to confinement and restraint as a first step when a student with a disability displays crisis behaviors, these are behaviors based in ignorance and fear that are at times exhibited in our modern world. Moreover, if we take a step even further back to the colonial and pre-colonial eras these abuses increase and we see more of people with disabilities being viewed as religious omens, animals, and worthy to be cast out of society.

It is important to understand this, not as an active definition of special education, but as an underlying understanding of the field because students with disabilities weren't even guaranteed a free and appropriate education until the mid-1970s with the Education for All Handicapped Children Act. All of this is the backdrop of our work as special educators. It is a quiet reminder for why this work exists and why it must be done well.

Our schools today

Today, the average school and modern education generally can be looked at from a number of different angles. It is about families, communities, and students. It is plagued by over-crowdedness, underfunding, and corruption. Teachers are undervalued, underdeveloped, and overworked. Education itself is undervalued by the populous and the work of education isn't given the proper reverence. It is about graduation, preparing the workforce, and milestones. It is also arguably the most political field of work that you could enter into outside of actual politics. Where special education sits within that framework is a very interesting place. The work of special education in a school effectively addresses the needs of the least in the school environment when it comes to indicators like management, development, and performance on state and district performance metrics.

Within a functional, well-adjusted, experienced, and qualified special education team a school should have at their disposal (among other things): the experts in behavior management, the experts in providing individualized support, the experts in differentiation, the experts in diverse learning needs and disability, the experts in collaboration, and the experts in effective intervention. When I was leading special education departments in schools some of the supports and trainings that I provided the school included new software integrations, training on collaborative teaching models, trainings on providing support to students with disabilities in a general education setting, pushing crisis intervention certification for teachers, and training on trauma-informed pedagogy. All of these extra supports and trainings that I provided faculties and classrooms in service of students and teachers were in no way things that I was instructed to do. They also weren't things that the school as an entity knew to do. There are a lot of different components of special education that you're exposed to when you've been in the profession long enough, and all of these best practices, strategies, and certifications aren't in the frame of reference of every school. Every special educator needs to on some level be pursuing expert status within their school on some level; and expert doesn't mean you need to be in school to get your PHD, it just means you're a person who is staying up to date on the latest strategies and you know what is proven to work based on the area of practice that you have interest. Every special educator needs to be comfortable saying to their department head or their administrator (granted they're not in a toxic work environment) these are the things that our students, our team, our school needs and these are the people who need them first. This is the attitude of a great special educator and a great special education team.

The problem with overcrowding in schools (besides it being more difficult to teach increasingly numerous students at once) is that only one student with a behavior issue has the power to change the educational outcomes of the entire class. On a daily basis they can derail lessons, distract teachers and students, influence student behaviors, and even create a toxic enough environment that the primary instructor starts to have medical issues. One good special educator can, for that student and that classroom, diagnose the issue, take ownership of it (particularly if it is a student with an IEP), remediate that student, and provide effective intervention to the extent that the entire narrative of that classroom changes and suddenly everyone in that classroom is learning and focused on a regular basis. When it comes to the yearly statewide performance metrics that every school needs to meet, they are often dragged down by the performance of students with disabilities who may struggle with academics and test taking. A good special educator should be able to identify the core services that the collection of students at the bottom end of those performance metrics need to show the growth the state is looking for. They're able to design instruction specifically for this general education expectation that will allow their students with disabilities to acquire the skills they lack. When it comes to classes that are too large, general instructors can become ill equipped to meet the level of differentiation needed to meet the diverse learning needs of their entire class effectively. A good special educator well versed in collaborative practices can go into a classroom and provide resources and support to the extent that no student is left behind during any part of the instructional cycle.

These are the things that good special educators can do. Special education (Tier 4) is the last stop of need and intervention in any school system; therefore, special educators need to be the most refined in the practice of intervention in the school building. Students can enter into special education for any number of needs (behavior, processing, physical needs, deficits, memory etc.). Special educators need to be adept to meet any number of needs, or at least know where they would go or what they would do in the cases in which a need arises. This is why it is so important for special educators to be seeking an expert status in their practice whatever it is and whenever they're doing it. You may be doing Co-teaching and you suddenly have to do small group classes. You may be accustomed to working with students with ADHD, but are suddenly given a student with autism. Special educators need to be flexible to meet the needs and/or create the value that their school building requires when it is needed. (Not even to mention the compliance)

Special education is greater than and more than what it is often assumed to be. It has to always be defined by the greatest extent of what it could be, and not by what has been the norm in any individual school building in the past. In a lot of poorly run schools, there is an adage from educators and special educators that they "just" do this or we "just" do that. That adage is somewhat about teacher confidence, but also largely about knowing evidence-based practices. If you "just" do anything in special education you're not doing the best work. It is important for special educators to have at the back of their minds and the forefront of their thoughts these definitions so that the work of special education can be done effectively, efficiently, and joyfully (because it can be very joyful work). All of this is important to keep you in the work of providing education and service to students with disabilities for the long haul.

Chapter 2: The Service Provider

What you'll notice about yourself as a special educator pretty much right away when you start the work is that you're going to be wearing many hats. Often this is truer for special educators than general educators because a special educator's work is more inherently individualized. A general education teacher can wear many hats, but most often only to the extent that the new hat can be generalized to a class of 30 students. Special educators on the other hand are expected to individualize their practices to whatever each individual student with a disability needs. They have to more or less become the avatar for that need in the classroom or in their school. In different schools that I've been a part of, I've seen special educators become parents, disciplinarians, coaches, crisis interventionists, substitutes, and social workers all in the course of one day. When a student on your caseload is in need at any point throughout the day, you may be (and often are) called up to support that student despite whatever your normal routine is. However, there are a couple of hats that a special educator cannot take off at any point in the day. There are hats that you cannot take on and off and place into the closet or your handbag for when it is convenient. The function of those essential hats are simply compliance and instruction. Now, you might be thinking that compliance and instruction are so obviously the roles that you have to maintain as a special educator that it doesn't need to be said, but these two functions happen to be the ones that are most undermined in schools when educators have multiple hats.

The primary functions of a special educator are undermined all the time in the name of wearing multiple hats. I've seen special educators walk into collaborative environments, a place where they are supposed to be teaching alongside a general instructor and suddenly, they're given the hat of best friend and babysitter to a disruptive student. They go into the classroom, sit directly next to a student that they know is going to interrupt instruction at some point, and overcorrect every behavior that this student exhibits. They'll chat with the student to build rapport, they'll redirect the student when they talk out or get up from their seat, they'll pull them into small groups, and they'll generally make sure that this student isn't a hindrance to instruction for the entire year. You might be asking yourself what's wrong with that. Well, best friend and babysitter aren't hats that a special educator needs to wear in lieu of being an instructor. While that teacher is sitting with that student all class-period, they are not being the instructor they're called to be. A collaborative teaching environment is one in which two teachers are working together to provide instruction to a group of students. This cannot be done if one of the instructors is solely focused on one disruptive student. Furthermore, collaborative or co-teacher services are usually provided to multiple students with disabilities at once. While that teacher is occupied with their one special friend, they are neglecting the instructional needs of the other students with disabilities sitting in that room. This is also true of the other general education students who should also be the beneficiaries of two teachers working together to deliver a lesson.

The disruptive student is also unable, in this case, to maximize their own capabilities in an environment where they should be receiving the least restriction. The Least Restrictive Environment (LRE) is a term used in special education that guides the determination of services. Special education students must be guaranteed the right to be in a learning environment with their same aged general education peers as much as possible. However, the LRE isn't exactly a place, but rather a guiding principle that determines how all services are provided and not merely where they're provided. In this case, if a special education student is in a general education environment, but requires so much support that a primary instructor has to sit with them the entire class period, they are likely not receiving an appropriate service. The student should be able to function in a similar fashion as their general education peers in that setting. So, either the special educator here is providing too much support and should be developing a plan to allow the student to behave appropriately in that setting without providing excessive amounts of attention or they need to revisit that student's documented services if that student cannot function without one-on-one support. In this way, this scenario also creates a compliance issue. If a special educator is in the classroom for collaborative or co-teaching services, but is providing one-on-one support, even if the general instructor is effectively managing the class, the other students with disabilities in the environment aren't getting the services outlined in their IEPs.

In this scenario (which is fairly common) it is very easy for special educators to neglect the primary functions of their work because they've been asked to put on other hats. Another fairly common one that you will see in collaborative spaces, is the teacher's assistant hat in which special educators aren't treated like actual teachers in that environment, but rather teacher's assistants. They'll be asked to pass out papers and grab copies during instruction (which I've always preempted gen ed teachers when we begin that co-teaching relationship that I'm not grabbing their copies). This can occur at the fault of a territorial gen ed teacher and even a lazy special education teacher. There are many different reasons and scenarios in which you may be wearing a hat that you didn't intend to wear as a special educator. Sometimes that is okay. However, it is important that you maintain the hats that support instruction and compliance at all times so that you always provide appropriate service to students with disabilities.

Now that we've discussed how wearing multiple hats can work as a special educator, we need to talk about, more importantly, which hats special educators need to wear at all times. In an effort to be always providing the right service, these hats must be maintained and never removed. These hats are service provider and case manager.

Service Provider and Case Manager

A service provider is a term that describes an individual who is the deliverer of the services outlined in a student's IEP. Services can range the gamut of things like one-on-one support, to co-teaching, to various forms of therapy. The person assigned to that service, which will also be outlined in the IEP, is the service provider. The service provider may be a therapist, a paraprofessional, and of course the special education teacher. As a service provider you are the person responsible for the delivery of the service outlined in the IEP. These are legally required services, so a service provider must at all times be aware that compliance isn't just tracking goals or delivering accommodations or even merely assessing the student, compliance is making sure that those services are rendered at the frequency and in the manner documented in the IEP. In many schools it is very common to have "funky" schedules. In these schedules there might be a lunch break or regular assembly in which a service provider's service hours are impacted. It is the job of that service provider, special educator, and special education department to review the schedule and IEP services to determine how to effectively provide the service to the student. If a student's IEP says they require 1 hour of special ed instruction in reading a day (which can always be revisited by the IEP team if that hour is not needed) and one of those days is impacted by a funky schedule, it is up to that service provider to take the lead in determining where that hour can be shifted to make sure that services are rendered. This is the level of scrutiny that a service provider must have in providing services to their students. An additional level of checks and balances on service providers comes from the case manager.

Case Managers

A Case Manager is the person assigned to a client who oversees all aspects of their care or services. In much the same fashion as what one would see in the healthcare industry or in social work, a special education case manager is the individual responsible for the reviewing, maintaining, and executing of the IEP and the services therein. They generally maintain all aspects of the educational program, communicate with stakeholders (including parents), and schedule meetings (usually IEP meetings) to maintain compliance. Most special education departments on your first day in the work, will have a caseload of students for whom you're the case manager. When it comes to services that the case manager is overseeing, especially in the case that they aren't providing those services directly as a special education teacher (which is often the case), they must make sure that those services are rendered.

It is very common to find that a service provider (due to neglect or disorganization), particularly in large school environments, has forgotten that they should be servicing a particular student during the day who may just be sitting in class at the other end of the building. It is the case manager's job to make sure that they are actively reviewing their case manager caseload to determine if services are being rendered, either by talking with the students or by checking in with each service provider periodically. Sometimes the flow of communication in school buildings comes from a department head rather than the case manager in many instances, but it is the case manager's responsibility to make sure that each service provider knows that they are or should be servicing their student. Sometimes this can be accomplished with a simple conversation with the service provider. If necessary, it can be a more direct ask like, "You're Blank's service provider. Can you start picking them up for instruction at this time on your schedule?". It is up to the case manager to determine how best to approach that discussion, and it is always best to come into these conversations with positivity and productivity, but this is ultimately the case manager's role.

Now that we cracked open a conversation on roles, there are a few aspects about the difference between a case manager and a service provider that are often missed to the detriment of students and teachers alike. It is incredibly common in fact to miss at least one of these items and if you are in a special education department right now and you don't understand one of these things I wouldn't be surprised. These things are so important in fact that instead of being poetic about it, I'm going to put them in a list so that they're clearer.

1. All Case Managers have a Case Management Caseload and a Full Caseload

In many professions that use the case manager system of linking professionals with clients to provide some service, that professional (for instance a social worker) will be the only social worker working with that client, which means they are providing all of the social work services. This is not the case for special education. Special Education often and usually requires one special educator to serve students to whom they aren't the case manager. In these cases, and for these students that special educator is a service provider. This means that this case manager has two caseloads. The Case Manager caseload is the caseload where the special educator is the case manager for all of the students. This means that the special educator is responsible for all of the communication, scheduling, and ensuring that services are provided to a student as they relate to the execution of an IEP. All special educators will also have a Full Caseload or Service Provider Caseload. This Full caseload is for every student that that special educator serves including: as a service provider, and as a case manager (as this is also a service).

This misconception, that special educators' caseloads don't include students that they're only the service provider to, is so rampant that I would guess that it has been true in more or less every school at least once. Because most special educators typically discuss their caseload in reference to their Case Manager caseload, and because it generally doesn't have a name, they aren't cognitively aware that they have two caseloads and the Full, or Service Provider, caseload will have more students that they must serve. As a result, students are often left underserved because their service providers may not pick them up for instruction (for instance), or even know that they're in the room in a collaborative teaching space. They also may not be aware of their accommodations right away or even things as basic as their disability. This occurs often at the fault of the special educator, but also at the fault of leadership who don't fully understand what the expectation should be.

Speech therapists, unlike many other types of service providers, are very common in schools (particularly elementary schools). They are responsible for every student in that school's speech/ language needs when it is required by an IEP. Therefore, they often end up being service provider to dozens of students. However, there are times in which that speech therapist is serving a student who only qualifies for speech, they don't have academic deficits that would require them to receive other special education services. In these cases, it is very common for that speech therapist to be responsible for all communication and services related to those few students, where she/he is the case manager, while also being responsible for the progress, goals and objectives, and interventions of the superior number of students who are also on her caseload for speech, but also have competing deficits or disabilities which qualify them for other special education services. The speech therapist is both case manager and service provider and all of these students together represent their full caseload. This is the same understanding that must exist in the special education departments of all schools.

2. Special Educators are responsible for each student on their full caseload

To segue from the last point, it is highly important that we discuss the implications and responsibilities of being a service provider versus being a case manager as sharing students or caseloads is a fairly regular occurrence in schools. Moreover, if special educators who take on the mantle of service provider don't take ownership of their full caseloads, they will undoubtedly be unraveling the progress they're attempting to nurture in students. The responsibilities of a special educator service provider include but are not limited to:

- ❖ Having a full knowledge of each student's accommodations
- ❖ Having a full knowledge of the goals and objectives related to the service they're providing for each student
- ❖ Having a working knowledge of each student's IEP
- ❖ Taking full responsibility for all aspects of the instruction (for that service) of that student during their service time
- ❖ Taking responsibility for the interventions that will be used to augment the student's progress and to meet their goals and objectives
- ❖ Making sure that the student is in attendance for their class
- ❖ Communicating with parents and the case manager when there are issues
- ❖ Being a part of the IEP team

One of the most frustrating things that can take place in schools is special educators who don't support other special educators. These are individuals who after getting a student added to their caseloads as a service provider, do not take the time to learn the needs of those students, forget that they need to be in their room for instruction, or otherwise don't take ownership of that student's needs because they're "not the case manager". Often, they have the attitude that if they aren't the case manager that they're doing a favor for the other special educator who is the case manager. The reality is, they aren't doing them a favor, they aren't even sharing caseloads, the school has assigned that special educator a student to add to their caseload as a service provider based on availability and compliance, and therefore they are responsible. That's it. This occurrence is unique to special educator service providers (therapists and other service providers tend to have a very clear understanding of what their role is) which is why it needs to end because this one misconception can break down any functioning special education department.

3. Service Provider are primary person responsible for goals and data collection

This next piece is related to the second point above, but needs to be separate because it is highly critical. The service provider is the primary individual responsible for the goals, data collection, and interventions related to the service they're providing to that student. It seems that it would rather intuitive that if you are the primary instructor for a student, you'd also be the primary person who should be supporting the determination of that students' progress in that particular area, but that is unfortunately not always the case. The service provider, in all cases, is the means by which a student shows growth in any particular area. If a student is behind in reading the service provider's job is to look at their goals, identify whatever instructional strategies they need to show growth, assess that growth on a regular basis, provide interventions if that student isn't responding appropriately to current practices, track the progress, and then report that progress and make appropriate suggestions for goals at that student's next IEP meeting. This is the case clearly and without question for therapists and other service providers, but in many of our schools there is a disconnect when it comes to the special education service provider. Usually this disconnect occurs around data collection.

Between the responsibilities of the case manager and the service provider, data collection can be the most cumbersome, because many schools and special education departments haven't standardized their data collection practices in a way that makes it easy to collect, record, and share data on a regular basis. These tasks are often left up to each special educator to decide. Consequently, there is no uniformity, and because the service provider is most often also the case manager for the student with a disability, they are usually the decider. Yet, when a student needs to be shared between caseloads the service provider (who isn't the case manager) will look to the case manager to collect all of the data even when that case manager isn't providing instruction. This should not be the practice.

Service providers need to be the primary entity that drives data collection and goal setting. In every school there is a division of labor and tasks. Regardless of who is actually printing or assessing each student, the service provider has to not only have access to that data for the purposes of goal setting and providing interventions, but also be the person to determine what assessments should be provided to the student. In any classroom, for any teacher, the person who is teaching the class should also be the person assessing progress and creating goals. (This is teaching 101) Yet somehow, in many places but not all, special educator service providers are giving that responsibility to the case manager, not looking at the data, and providing "general instruction" for that service content area, not leading the setting of goals in the IEP (since the case manager can technically do that too), and consequently the team wonders why the student isn't showing the progress they're looking for in that service area.

These things are very important to the service provide and can be done simply enough. If a special educator or a special education team spends enough time on the front end (during the first month of the school year) setting up the systems that are going to make data collection and providing service effective and easy; you won't have to be constantly battling with that requirement of your role throughout the school year. If you find yourself struggling in this area (trying to figure out how to assess, collect, record, and share data) at the end of the school year, someone has dropped the ball. However, no matter how difficult it may appear it doesn't excuse the service provider from their responsibility.

A good service provider can incorporate all of these understandings into their practice. Special educator service providers should be able to execute all of the functions of a seasoned teacher and all of the functions of related service providers like therapists. They are instructing, intervening, communicating, setting goals, participating, and generally taking ownership of students for their assigned service area.

Chapter 3: Collaboration

Team work makes the dream work! We're family! Sharing means caring! ... and other aphorisms that you hear often when working in schools. They are true enough. You cannot get anything done within a school environment unless you engage in some level of collaboration which is what all of these phrases point to. From lesson planning to the rotation of grade level chair responsibilities educators need to collaborate. Collaboration is key because a teacher doesn't have all of the skills and tools necessary to do a great job on their own. Teaching is a practice just like law and medicine. You can't do the work effectively if you don't collaborate throughout your career to gain knowledge and find new solutions, solutions that often come from other people. Teaching isn't just your classroom; it is your school, an entire ecosystem. The school and the professionals therein are the primary vehicle by which you will collaborate and solidify your teaching practice. This is true of all teachers, but this is even more true for special educators because special educators are case managers. Yes, general education teachers will do things like plan meetings and speak with service providers, but as we've reviewed in the previous chapter, special educators will be asked to do an array of tasks on a systematic level for students with disabilities that regular ed teachers will generally not be required to do. So, the reason why collaboration is important for special educators is because the practice of special education is significantly more complex than general education. Not to say that general educators have an easier job, they don't, but the work they must do is not as complex as a special educator's.

Special educators have to plan, tack, review, and document so many different types of items while being the experts in their buildings in disability and education. Furthermore, many of the items special educators need to take ownership of exist outside of the framework of simply getting in front of students and teaching. This is why working collaboratively is highly critical to the special educator. There are three primary entities that the special educator needs to be able to collaborate with successfully to meet the needs of students: the Special Education Department, Stakeholders, and General Education Teachers.

The Special Education Department

I've been in special education for a while and have seen many different school environments, and I can tell you without any reservation that the difference between a successful special education department (one that is successfully meeting the needs of students with disabilities) and one that isn't successful is collaboration. You cannot do the work of special education without collaborating with the people on your team. Even if you're inept at every other aspect of your job, you will still be somewhat successful if you are able to collaborate with your special education department. Now, before I get into what a collaborative special education department looks like I'm going to review what fake collaboration is in SPED. The reason for this is because you may be bedazzled, mesmerized, and entranced by the ways in which many dysfunctional departments feign effective collaboration.

Fake Collaboration

- Having Department Meetings every week
- Providing breakfast to your team
- Bringing in goody bags when it is a team member's birthday
- Signing greetings cards
- Having a secret Santa
- Holiday Potlucks
- Sharing a resource room/ learning space
- Sharing students
- Scolding another teacher's unruly students
- Attending another teacher's IEP meetings

Now you may be asking yourself, "I would love to have some of this in my school. What's wrong with these things?" The reason why this is evidence of fake collaboration is because none of these practices in and of themselves will improve your practice as a special educator. Now, mind you it is a wonderful thing to have a department that believes in motivation and morale. We all know how sparing morale is in education as a whole. I've seen many successful departments that do their best to show they care for their colleagues and students by exhibiting these behaviors, but these behaviors won't necessarily produce good special educators or good departments. They're wonderful to do, and you can certainly enhance the functionality of your department by doing them, but by themselves they won't improve compliance or effective teaching.

Even if you ignore the items that are centered specifically around morale and building a positive culture (which is good) like potlucks and greeting cards, others of the more job focused practices don't necessarily produce the end goal of better collaboration. We can use the examples of having special education department meetings every week and attending another teacher's IEP meetings. Special education department meetings are a means of disseminating information and assuring compliance. Full attendance doesn't mean collaboration. Agreeing on the department's norms, rules, and expectations doesn't mean collaboration. Turning to IEP meetings, as a special educator who's also a service provider, you are responsible for every student you serve, so attending an IEP by itself is the bare minimum of your responsibility.

Effective collaboration, a collaboration that seeks to improve the practices of special educators and provide the highest value to students with disabilities, within a special education department is about engagement and investment in your colleagues' knowledge, you own development, and the development of the department as a whole. There's a saying that I heard when I first entered special education that went something like, "Just assume I'm right, it saves time." Special educators are often so busy they don't have time to debate or discuss items that are of low priority or those that already have a working solution when there is usually so much to do already. Yet, this is exactly why collaboration is so important. There is no curriculum for the special educator, there is no team lesson plan, there is only a living document called an IEP. Special educators must often, but also don't have the time to design everything from scratch every time they get a new student or start a new school year. They have to actively be thinking about: What am I going to need in a week, a month, by the end of the year; How can I make sure this service provider has what they need to meet my student's needs according to the IEP; These systems aren't working for me, how can we do this better? Unless a special educator is consistently goal oriented, looking to improve the practices of themselves and others on their team, and actively trying to improve their knowledge repository they will always have issues in their work. All of these are aspects of collaboration in a special education department. One of the most frustrating things you may hear in a special education department is, "I just google it" or "You should just google" in response to a question about how anything is done or what resources are used. This is an indication that something may be wrong in your department and that intentional collaboration is not taking place.

Here is what collaboration actually looks like in a special education department:

Good Collaboration

o   Having team members present new and useful training to their department
o   Providing breakfast to special education students to support their engagement in the program
o   Bringing supplies to another teacher who may need them
o   Designing programs to support IEP parents
o   Sharing new student software programs for the classroom
o   Sharing students' assessment results
o   Generalizing behavior expectations for students so that they're followed the same way for each teacher

- Creating goals and objectives for all students you service
- Offering to calling parents for a shared student
- Advocating to your administration on behalf of your team
- Looking for professional development opportunities
- Sharing data collection methods
- Sharing data collection results
- Supporting your team's completion of compliance/ certification assessments
- Collecting behavior data on challenging students
- Offering your space as a quiet place to work during planning periods
- Offering to administer assessments or probes for your colleagues
- Helping with classroom décor
- Providing access to unique accommodations
- Helping colleagues' study for certification exams

These are the behaviors that are going to help students and improve your practice. The goal of collaboration in schools is to serve the student. Although I'm a strong proponent of the belief that a good teacher is a happy teacher, if your collaboration is based solely on attendance and morale you aren't going to have a strong impact on the student. All of the above practices will be very helpful and I encourage you to find and research more ways to be of use to your own practice and your colleagues, which mutually is essentially what collaboration is. However, I think the greatest litmus test for effective collaboration in a special education department is the student (and this is true of really any classroom). If you ask the student "who helps you?" they will answer you honestly, and they should be able to say this for every service provider and special educator they're in contact with. And even in the case that they aren't doing work with a particular member of your special education team; they should be able to generalize behavior expectations to anyone within your department when they enter the room (which they will do even if you don't ask them when you guide them appropriately). Do they recognize that educator as a valuable member of your teacher team, someone to be respected? A good question for students, and a good question for yourself, is what value am I bringing to my department?

Stakeholders

Stakeholders are another important group that all special education professionals need to cater to in their practice of collaboration. Stakeholders in this context is anyone who is not a teacher, in or outside of a school, that has input or stake in an IEP or in the life of the student with an IEP. Stakeholders can be virtually anyone including: parents, grandparents, therapists, doctors, lawyers, law enforcement officers, school administrators, coaches, advocates, siblings, and counselors. Depending on their level of involvement in the IEP process they can be highly important to your work and someone that you need to interact with regularly to provide adequate value to a student, or someone that you only need to be in contact with once a year. The stakeholders that you will always be in contact with are parents and guardians. Parents and guardians should be your highest priority in terms of stakeholders for any student.

They are the ones you will communicate with the most and the ones that have the most influence over the IEP process as they have the right to continue, challenge, and revoke services for their child. It is always best to be in contact with parents or guardians routinely and frequently based upon need. Providing to them sufficient information to understand their rights and the needs of their child, respecting their time, listening to their concerns, and directly making appropriate asks of them is highly important to maintaining a good relationship with parents. These are the same practices that you must apply when interacting with all stakeholders to the extent in which you need to interact with them as they will likely require less communication than parents/guardians.

Service providers at times can also be considered stakeholders for a student with an IEP. Oftentimes, these service providers, be they therapists or counselors, don't have a working space within your school building which means they aren't members of your special education department. In these cases, that service provider should be treated with the same level of deference as other stakeholders.

There are a lot of horror stories out there when it comes to interacting with stakeholders in the IEP process because they can often be perceived as needy and can make educational decision-making take longer, but the thing that is important to keep in mind is that they're doing what they do in service of the student. I've seen and heard of many a disgruntled stakeholder, like parents or advocates, that gums up a meeting (Special education is also a highly litigious department of education which we will review later in this survival guide), however, I've had little to know significant problems when it has come to the stakeholders that I'm required to interact with. I can ascribe this success to three primary attributes: preparedness, openness, and honesty. If you remain prepared, open, and honest when you're interacting with your stakeholders you will most likely be successful in your collaboration efforts because these are highly important aspects of having a solutions orientation. Parents/ Guardians and other stakeholders want to solve problems as much as you do, so if you can remain prepared for things you are responsible for, open to listening and being flexible, and be honest about your thoughts and feelings about the best way to move forward you can win them over to your side. You can help them help you do your job easier as a case manager. As a case manager, you're not there to trick parents into caring less about their child so that you don't have to do as much paperwork. You are not there to disguise the deficits of a student because you don't want an advocate to request additional services. Your job is to solve problems. In special education, if you aren't solving problems you're most likely creating more.

General Education Teachers

The last and most important collaborative relationship that the special educator is charged to collaborate with is the general education teacher. General education teachers are by far the most difficult group of people to collaborate with on almost every level which is why collaborating with them takes the most time, the most attention, and the most planning. Before I explain what you might be facing, and how to collaborate successfully in a special educator/ general educator relationship, I'm going to give you some examples of things I've either witnessed, experienced, or heard when a special educator is required to collaborate with a general education teacher just so that we're on the same page:

- A special education is told by a gen ed teacher the when they enter the room, they can pull a group of students to the back of the room and goes over whatever the gen ed teacher is working on with the majority of the class
- Gen ed teacher refuses to provide a student with an IEP read aloud accommodations during instruction because they "are busy with too many students"
- Gen Ed teacher regularly neglects to share lesson plans so that they can be modified for the special education students
- Special educator sits with a student with an IEP all class period instead of helping deliver instruction
- Gen Ed teacher neglects to gather any work samples for a student for the entire month prior to that student's annual IEP review
- Gen ed teacher consistently asks special educator to run copies during instruction
- Special educator is forced to do all of the instruction while present in the room, gen ed teacher sits down and answers questions
- Gen ed teacher refuses to engage in the instruction while the special educator is presenting
- Special educator doesn't review how to provide accommodations to students after handing over a list of accommodations to the teacher
- Gen ed teacher refuses to provide accommodations at all
- Gen ed teacher leaves all parent contact to the special educator

❖ Gen ed teacher talks about the special educator behind their back to other teachers and says they're "in the way" during co-teaching
❖ Gen ed teacher refuses to be flexible to accommodate their student when the special ed teacher has IEP related priorities during the instructional hour that has impacted their schedule
❖ Gen ed teacher uses collaborative instructional time to take breaks and use the bathroom
❖ Gen ed teacher sends the student with an IEP to the special educator's office any time there is an issue instead of trying to solve the problem
❖ Gen ed teacher continually yells and berates a student with a behavior disorder instead of following the prescribed plan for interaction in their behavior intervention plan

By far and away, the relationship that the special educator has with the general education instructor can be the most fraught and tenuous. There is no shortage of examples of how the good work of special education has been undermined by poor gen education teacher relationships to the detriment of students. When they're not good they can run the gamut of inconvenient to nasty and unprofessional at the fault of either party. However, maintaining a positive relationship and a productive relationship can be achieved with some rather common collaborative tools. Before we review these tools, it is important to discuss the types of relationships that you will primarily have with the general education teacher. Below you will find of a description of these relationships and what tools can be used to maintain them.

The Case Management Relationship

The case management relationship is one in which the special educator is reaching out to the general education teacher to discuss or get support for a student on their caseload (Case Manager caseload or Full/Service caseload). As a case manager, you might be looking for an update on the student's progress, looking to review a new accommodation with the teacher so that it can be implemented in the general education setting, asking for the teacher to fill out a form to explain what the student's current needs are for evaluation, or simply inviting that teacher to an upcoming IEP meeting. This is the most typical relationship that a special educator will have with a general education teacher because regardless of what grade band you're teaching, any student can have between 4-9 instructors on average. So, although the case management relationship takes less time on a daily basis, due to the number of teachers that may have input on a student, this type of relationship will take some careful monitoring. No matter what that teacher teaches (be it a core subject or a special class like art) they are teacher stakeholders for the student and therefore that relationship is important regardless of what it requires. It is important to also remember that this relationship requires advocacy. The special educator is the expert in the IEP for the student with a disability to the general educator. So, to the extent that the gen ed teacher needs to be providing different or better instruction to the student with a disability, a positive and open case management relationship needs to be established so that the gen ed teacher responds appropriately to the needs of the student when the special educator asks.

Below are some strategies and best practice that you can use to maintain a productive case management relationship with your general education teachers:

Best Practices for the Case Management Relationship

- ❖ Create trust with that teacher by providing them with all accommodations and relevant documentation (like behavior plans) related to the student with an IEP as early as possible
- ❖ Provide any updates to accommodations or services as soon as possible
- ❖ Ask for their feedback on the progress of and general adaptability of the student with an IEP to educational expectations
- ❖ Offer support with integrating accommodations into the general education setting
- ❖ Support the general education teacher with contacting parents
- ❖ Ask the general education teacher about information related to how the students is effectively transitioning between educational settings
- ❖ Express your gratitude toward the general educator for supporting the student with a disability

Collaborative or Co-Teaching Relationship

The collaborative or co-teaching relationship is one in which a special educator is joining a general education class to provide instruction alongside that general educator. The difference between collaborative and co-teaching is generally defined by the length of time in which the special educator is teaching with the general educator in the general education setting. If a special educator is in the classroom for less than a full segment of instruction (the special educator joins the classroom after instruction for a subject has begun or if that special educator leaves the classroom before instruction for a subject has concluded) it is considered collaborative teaching. If that special educator is in the classroom with the general education teacher for the entire instructional segment for a subject it is referred to as co-teaching. Although these relationships are very similar as they will require the same types of tools to maintain them, they do require different levels of preparation to ensure that instruction is effectively provided to all of the students in the classroom. These relationships take the most time to effectively manage.

Below are some practices that will keep a collaborative or co-teaching relationship functioning effectively, however, before you review these practices, please keep in mind that co-teaching isn't just a relationship, it is a skill. Every co-teacher should have either been trained in or exposed to co-teaching methodologies and models. It is a very common misconception that the extent of co-teaching is teaching at the same time or splitting the class up in two different groups. This is not the case. Co-teaching and collaborative teaching and its practical application is more sophisticated than any individual teacher can glean from an indirect exposure to it. If you are a special educator or general educator that knows they will be working in some type of collaborative model and neither of you have ever been trained, you need to ask your administration to provide you collaborative/co-teaching training as soon as possible.

Best Practices for the Collaborative/ Co-teaching Relationship

- ❖ Schedule a weekly planning session with your co-instructor to review the needs of the classroom and reflect on the classes progress
- ❖ Request general lesson plans to be forwarded to the special educator prior to the beginning of the week so that they can include or suggest appropriate accommodations for students with disabilities
- ❖ Set time aside to get to know your co-instructor through things like text or by sharing a meal
- ❖ Establish clear roles considering the instructional needs of all students and the instructional needs of students with disabilities
- ❖ Agree upon and participate equally in a classroom management system
- ❖ Establish and model a shared and equal authority with the students
- ❖ Discuss your strengths, weaknesses, and pet peeves
- ❖ Create effective channels for communication like text, email, message boards, phone calls etc.
- ❖ Establish an open non-judgmental relationship that promotes honesty, trust, and flexibility
- ❖ Cater the instructional delivery to the needs of the lesson and allow each other occupy novel roles within the lesson
- ❖ Create effective routines

Collaborative types of teaching are the most difficult to implement, but they can be the most rewarding. There is nothing better in the difficult work that is teaching to have someone else in the room that you trust and even admire to support and assess the students, manage behaviors, and otherwise share the workload. My most successful co-teaching relationship started out fairly rocky. There was no trust and there were a lot of hurt feelings, but when you take the time to get to know a person, like I started doing, things can turn around. Education can be a very isolating profession and educators like to feel like they have someone on their side. Taking the time to share a meal, talk about current events, and lessen each other's workloads can go a long way in building rapport and having a productive relationship. However, collaborative practices aren't good to know and implement because they're helpful or even fun, they're essential because they're here to stay.

With the rise of overcrowding in schools and coupled with a very well documented teacher shortage across the United States, classrooms are not getting smaller, they're getting larger. Collaboration is becoming more essential to manage and maintain our educational system while the standards held to teachers only increase. In and outside of the classroom, teachers need to be able to (and should expect to) collaborate effectively with their colleagues. Special educators in particular have to do this with a number of stakeholders all of which are necessary to provide students with disabilities the appropriate access to their educations. Furthermore, when we think of collaboration, we have to remember that teaching is a practice and therefore cannot be done without collaboration. You have to ask yourself what are my spheres of influence and who exists in those spheres so that you can leverage those relationships to provide the maximum value to your work.

Chapter 4: Advocacy

The number one thing that most lay people understand about special education is that special education is for people with disabilities. They also recognize certain features of the field like the use of short buses and the special education classroom, where they may believe all of the special education students are housed. The landscape of special education now is however very different from how it possibly is or was perceived. Students with disabilities today can be found all over school buildings in various different settings. Much of that reality was created in the special education law that was passed through IDEA, and the concept of least restrictive environment, a term that guides the creation of IEPs and endeavors to make sure that all students with disabilities are receiving services in environments that are the least restrictive to their educational needs. In this chapter we will be reviewing the vehicle through which that change occurs and explore how we actually get students in the right setting with the right services and accommodations.

Special education isn't as simple or as easy as saying this is the service that I believe this student should have, let's get him/her that service. It isn't even as simple as using data to support your findings on the student in many cases, and using that to guide decision making. Oftentimes, what service a student with disabilities receives and the manner in which they receive that service is often dictated (from a practical sense) by politics and financial feasibility. Sometimes administrators will push back on services because they're viewed as too costly or too much of a burden on the faculty. Sometimes services can be delayed, suspended, or deferred for logistical reasons even after a decision has been approved. In these hypothetical (but also probably regularly occurring) scenarios the only way to provide access and value to the student with a disability is through advocacy.

Advocacy is making public support or recommendations for the best interests of a person or entity. In the previous chapter we reviewed a little about how advocacy is related to the relationship that a special educator has with a general educator, but the role in which advocacy plays in the work of special education is far deeper and broader than this. A special educator has to be an advocate for the student with a disability, their families, and the future of that student in and outside of the classroom as the goal of an IEP is not only to make a plan for the student's current grade, but the create a functional roadmap for how that student matriculates and enters the community as an adult with a disability.

Now, let me preface this chapter and what will be covered in this chapter by saying that advocacy is probably the least understood and poorly executed skill of the special educator in general which is why in many ways it is not often displayed. It would not be a surprise that even after reading this entire survival guide that you, as a special educator, still struggle with this skill. Advocacy in special education requires a certain level of competence in some of the harder skills in the work like writing IEPs and data collection, yet in and of itself is a soft skill. Moreover, like all advocates, the work of advocacy is often thwarted by conflicting interests.

Special educators like many teachers are often driven by that which requires the least amount of work on their part. Sometimes the advocacy of a special educator comes second to the desire to do less paperwork or "make it" to the next scheduled break, and so they'll provide adequate service or acceptable accommodations in lieu of programs and services that are more robust or effective because they may require more paperwork or planning. Special educators may also work in service of themselves. One of the most tragic realities of the current teaching industry is that many teachers as soon as they enter the classroom are in a race to get out of the classroom to obtain a cushy high salaried non-teaching role with of course copious breaks. Now, on face value this may mean that they're interested in doing the best job possible when it comes to their work, but in reality, when it comes to advocacy this can often mean that they're willing to sacrifice needs or interests of students with disabilities and parents in support of administrations that feel certain services are too costly and families are too time consuming or inconvenient.

Special educators have to be in service of the student at all times. Furthermore, being in service of the student or an advocate at all times doesn't mean being an advocate for merely the IEP as it exists. I've read dozens and dozens of IEPs from a number of different school systems and different states and the reality is that they don't always reflect the current functioning of the student as they should. Whether it be by mistake or intentionally giving no thought to whether accommodations are still appropriate year after year, a special educator who is an advocate is constantly validating and revalidating their IEPs. They're looking to identify if this service, accommodation, or descriptions in the

IEP are still relevant. I've seen IEPs that are wildly inaccurate to the student. They may report something like the student is 5 years behind in reading fluency when in reality they're only 2 and the only reason that narrative is repeated is because the student hates test taking and actively tries to fail unless they're being assessed one on one. It doesn't take a genius to figure that out, but as a result that student may be, semester after semester, placed in remedial classes that they don't need and given accommodations that don't work. Special educators often perpetuate issues like this because it is inconvenient to have a meeting, do paperwork, and conduct an amendment IEP. However, no matter how inconvenient it is, it is completely necessary. What is at stake when we aren't advocating for students and validating the documentation we finalize in the IEP is the student being passed on to other case managers, to other teachers and systems who end up receiving inaccurate information, which keeps them from being able to effectively serve the student. Following IEPs that haven't been validated, have been copied and pasted year after year, that haven't included a relevant assessment of the student since their initial evaluation can set students back years.

Some of the primary ways in which a special educator can effectively provide value to a student through advocacy can be captured in the following:

- ❖ Checking to see if accommodations are being provided in each class
- ❖ Talking to stakeholders about their questions or concerns about the student
- ❖ Reviewing student progress with service providers
- ❖ Making sure parents are reviewing documentation and recommendations

- ❖ Asking administrators for support with different components of the IEP
- ❖ Making sure service providers have the proper training to support the student
- ❖ Making sure the student understands their own accommodations
- ❖ Explaining medical needs for the student to all stakeholders
- ❖ Assessing the student to validate their current level of need
- ❖ Talking to case managers about recommendations for future IEP services

The above is by no means an exhaustive list. There are innumerable ways in which you as a special educator can advocate for your students. However, what is important to recognize about any type of advocacy is that you have to advocate to all stakeholders at all times. You have to be an advocate for the student, yes, but to parents, lawyers, doctors, gen ed teachers, service providers, paraprofessionals, and any other person that is in contact with a student with a disability to the extent that that relationship can or will impact their educational outcomes. If there is a bus driver or a lunch lady who is impacting your student's outcomes, a good special educator will find a way to advocate to those people when appropriate. Some stakeholders are easy to communicate with and advocate to, but others take more time. Special educators have to be willing to take some time, be direct, have a conversation, and end it with a shared vision of how together they will support the student.

The last and arguably the most important person that a special educator needs to advocate to is the student themselves. Students don't necessarily, regardless of their age, have the competence or perspective to know what's best for them in an educational setting or what behaviors will lead them to the outcomes that they desire. Even adults need counseling and therapy at times. Moreover, their objectives in school may be different than what is prescribed to them in the IEP. I've seen so many students in different schools who go the entire year exhibiting a behavior that is completely inappropriate (academically or physically) and not a single professional will check them for it. Academically they might be refusing to open their text book during instruction because they struggle with reading, so they only listen to the teacher. Oftentimes the student may earnestly believe this is appropriate because they may have a reading-related disability and it might be harder to follow along when reading as a group. However, our job as special educators is to get students to overcome their disabilities with their strengths. So, not to require a student to follow along when reading as a group is to say their disability is immutable and cannot be circumvented with best practices, to say perhaps someone with dyslexia cannot learn to read in a group. This is not true. This is to the detriment of students.

Behaviorally, a student might be rolling balls throughout the classroom during instruction. They may have been given the ball appropriately as a stress reliever for a behavior related disability, but are now using that item regularly to disrupt the learning of themselves and others because they're bored or it tickles them. To not address that behavior, and to not remove that item as their accommodation in the moment, is to say that students with disabilities are not responsible for their behaviors and furthermore the item used to fulfill the accommodation is immutable. The ball usually isn't the accommodation, but rather the accommodation should read something like "stress reliever" or "manipulative". Even if the accommodation reads "ball" (which it shouldn't) the accommodation doesn't dictate, what ball, which ball, or when. That accommodation could be easily replaced with a bigger ball, a smaller ball, or one you can't roll across the room. When a student with a disability isn't held to account because of their disability, when they're not properly advocated to, we start to write IEPs around the disability rather than the student with the disability.

The conversations that should be held with students with disabilities to discuss their progress and current functioning should be happening on a, not necessarily frequent, but routine basis. It should be something that they expect from you. A good way to start that conversation with the student is this:

> "Hi (Student). I wanted to talk to you today about your progress. I see how you've been improving in (area of growth) on your test scores. I'm very proud of you for that. However, I've also noticed some things that I think we should address to make sure you're on the right track. Although you always complete your tests, during your class assignments I notice that you regularly turn in incomplete work. I've also noticed that you put your head down during class at least twice each class period. Do you know why you're doing this? I'd like to help you address this so that it doesn't continue to impact your progress."

After you've had this conversation, not only will you find a solution that you and the student can work on together, but the student will also acknowledge you as a person who will be regularly assessing their behavior and progress. This is a very important dynamic. Most teachers don't have a lot of time to address individual behaviors in an intentional way, usually just in the moment as a correction or toward the end of a grading period. Case managers and special educators have a greater opportunity to address their students' needs more frequently and with more intentionality. These types of conversations should be happening as needed and as regularly as once a month. Special educators have the tendency (like other teachers) to address poor behaviors once they've gotten out of hand, and usually through reprimand and yelling. This is a bad idea. Besides the fact that students with disabilities have disabilities and yelling isn't a therapeutic service to create lasting change, when things are out of hand students are usually at a heightened emotional state and are not receptive to behavior modification. They may stop in the moment, but what's not happening is them learning to self-correct, them learning to be solution oriented, or self-aware. They may also not internalize what was said because they're responding emotionally to your anger not intellectually to a redirection.

Advocacy is in many ways the defining feature of the special education practice. The paperwork and the compliance are most often done behind the scenes (which is often why it can be done poorly as well), but what we see on a daily basis that looks different than what other teachers do in the classroom is advocacy. It isn't providing accommodations, as general educators have to do this as well. It isn't working in small groups, because general educators have to do this at times as well. It is about proactively and preemptively walking the halls and observing, talking to stakeholders and teachers about the student with the disability, having age-appropriate conversations with student about their needs and progress, and truly moving the ball forward in terms of having the student gain access to their educations and their futures.

This means validating every aspect of the student's performance and their educational program. There are indicators of this advocacy on a compliance level. In the past I've had a full caseload of over 30 students (this is highly uncommon), but to get each of these students what they needed I had to adjust and validate how we recorded their progress and services on their IEP. This often meant that some students would have multiple IEP meetings or conferences throughout the year. Even on a typical caseload for highly effective special educators, I would find it hard to believe that not a single student required an amendment or some kind of additional meeting outside of their annual review meeting to adjust or validate services. If this isn't taking place at all, it might be an indicator that advocacy isn't taking place at the level that it should be.

Advocacy isn't a skill that can be assessed or taught very easily. However, it is every special educator's responsibility to be thinking about, "is this student receiving the best services?" and, for every issue that springs up from that student's case, "is there a plan in place for this?". Waiting a year to revisit a student's progress is often not good enough. Allowing natural consequences to occur for a student who curses at teachers regularly (like a suspension), is not a plan for addressing that behavior. If the student is coming into school exhausted every day, you may need to advocate to the parent. If the school doesn't have the right assistive technology for the student, you might need to advocate to the principal. Advocacy isn't easy and it may not even be a natural way to think for some people, but every great special educator should embody advocacy as a formal disposition of their work.

Chapter 5: The Legal

So far in this survival guide I've provided a brief introduction to the laws that govern special education. There are only a few primary laws that practically govern and assure the provision of special education services particularly to the extent that special educators should be actively aware of them. Those are IDEA, FAPE, and FERPA. In this chapter we'll be dissecting these laws and provisions to paint a better picture of why students with disabilities are entitled to certain services and what aspects of how special education is provided is ensured by these laws. We'll also be discussing how a special educator should practically understand these laws as an aspect of their work. Practically, understanding these laws, even on a simplistic level, should represent the why behind how services in all of their manifestations are provided to students with disabilities.

FAPE

Although the majority of what most come to understand about special education is provided by IDEA (Individuals with Disabilities Education Act), FAPE, Free and Appropriate Public Education, is somewhat of a precursor to IDEA. It essentially represents the provision that ensures all students with disabilities an education, and as the name describes a "free", "appropriate", and "public" one. The provision of FAPE was guaranteed by the Rehabilitation Act of 1973. It was designed essentially to ensure that the status of having a disability did not exclude students from the entitlement of their educations.

The reason why special educators should be aware of FAPE is because to the extent that students are not being provided with that entitlement, you as a special educator need to be able to advocate for or defend the provision of FAPE that you and/or your school is providing. In some of the examples that were provided in previous chapters I may have mentioned circumstances in which a student with a disability isn't being provided appropriate service. These could be situations in which the provision of FAPE is not being provided with efficacy. If a school regularly schedules activities which impact the learning of students with disabilities, but not others, special educators must be aware of the fact that this might be impacting the student's provision of FAPE. The correct response in this case would be to question or review that schedule with a supervisor to ensure that the students are receiving that adequate service.

In 2014, a complaint was filed by the Department of Education, Office of Civil Rights, against the Bay Village City School district. The complaint alleged that students with disabilities were being subjected to a shortened school day as a result of transportation and administrative convenience. The claim suggested that because the students in special education were being dismissed from school 10 minutes early on a regular basis, they were not receiving a full school day of instruction and therefore their provision of FAPE was being undermined. Resultantly, the school district decided to settle the complaint out of court prior to the completion of a full investigation issuing direction throughout their system that the school day for students with disabilities is not to be shortened, as the complaint suggests, for transportation and administrative convenience.

This and other cases are brought before courts every year to challenge schools who as an institution have neglected the rights and entitlements of students with disabilities. This is important for special educators to be aware of because it is easy (and often common) to overlook the rights of students with disabilities because their programming requires more effort and planning to implement effectively. A free and appropriate public education may not be terms in which a special educator may intuitively think, however, they should be asking themselves "is my student/s being excluded from or denied certain or any rights or privileges that general education students enjoy simply because of their disability or the complexity of their education program?".

In schools they may be denied recess because it conflicts with one of their services in the schedule, or they may be ineligible for a school-wide enrichment system because they spend the day in the special education setting. These may not conflict with the provision of FAPE, particularly in the way that denying that student a special class like gym would be as a punishment, however when these things occur the proper attitude of the special educator would be to identify and assure the ways in which school decisions can or will impact the special education student. When the school administrator announces at a faculty meeting the implementation of a new STEM program, the correct response would be to ask how will the students with disabilities be able to participate in it.

It is also important to recognize the "public" aspect of this provision. It has been relevant from time to time when it comes to how private schools provide special education services to understand that FAPE may not at times apply to the students in those schools in the same way. The provision of special education is always trickier when it comes to private schools. Some private schools may not have a robust special education program and their services might be limited. Also, how a student enrolls at a private school may determine what services they're provided. If a private school placement is a decision made by a public-school IEP team due to that institution being the best place for that student to receive FAPE, they may acquire a full range of services in that institution at no cost to the parent. However, if a parent pulls the student out of special education in the public school and then wishes to enroll the student in a private school because it may have better teachers or more resources, that student may not receive the same services they would with an IEP in a public school even if generally the private school is a better learning environment. This of course is not legal advice. I would always suggest to parents that if they want to leave the public school system to consult a lawyer if the provision of special education is something that they have identified as being important when, if, and when they move their child to the private school of their own volition.

IDEA

The Individual with Disabilities Education Act was originally known as the Education for all Handicapped Children's act which was enacted in 1975. The act went through multiple subsequent iterations, but its most prominent change was signed into law in 2004 by President George W. Bush which provided major amendments that fundamentally changed the way in which education is provided to students with disabilities. IDEA is broken into 4 primary parts. Part A reviews the general provisions of the act. This includes recognition of the history of special education, what research says about why and how it should be applied, and even acknowledgement of the reality of disproportionality in special education. It also includes definitions like what a student with a disability is and what the services provided to them are. Part B reviews the provision of FAPE in the least restrictive environment. Part C reviews provisions to infants and toddlers and their families. Part D reviews federal grants that can assist and support the provision of special education and its stakeholders.

Practically, the primary aspects of special education that a teacher should be aware of within IDEA are the provision of FAPE, the Least Restrictive Environment (LRE), the Individualized Education Program (IEP), Assessments, Transition Services, Parental Rights and Teacher Participation, and Discipline. We've introduced most of these concepts already in your survival guide, but we'll be reviewing them again in more detail

In lieu of being overly verbose about the legality and specific provisions of these components, the best ways for special educators to conceptualize these components so that they are applicable in their daily practice in education is in the following:

- **FAPE**: Making sure that students with disabilities are receiving appropriate educations on par with those provided to general education students.
- **LRE**: With consideration to their disability, making sure a student's services in special education aren't restricting their access or ability

to perform in a manner that is comparable to their general education peers without limitation.

- **IEP**: A living document, the program through which a student with a disability is provided special education services and ensured access to the general curriculum.
- **Transition Services**: Making sure that all planning and programming documented in an IEP is in service of the future in which the student with a disability is independent or no longer receiving special education services as they matriculate.
- **Parental Rights and Teacher Participation**: Ensuring all teachers are compliant with the appropriate roles and processes related to the IEP and parents are knowledgeable and aware of their rights and privileges.
- **Discipline**: Being proactively aware of the legal constraints of schoolwide discipline on students with disabilities to provide appropriate intervention and consultation.

It doesn't require a degree in law to be a special educator, but to have a baseline understanding of how IDEA, and other types of legislation that impact the lives of students with disabilities, works is not only accessible but important to the practice of special education. When it comes to questions about how one should serve and guide parents, advocate to general educators, advise administrators (who in many cases generally lack expertise in special education), or craft a cohesive IEP document, having an understanding of these components that come directly from IDEA will allow special educators to do their work in an effective and confident manner.

FERPA

The Family Educational Rights and Privacy Act (FERPA) is designed to ensure a parent's and in certain cases a student's right to access, review, inspect, modify, or overall correct a student's educational records. It also captures the general privacy and confidentiality in which these records should be treated. This law is in fact applicable to all students regardless of whether or not they have a disability, but this is an important part of special education because IEPs are educational records and therefore need to be protected in this way. Although this law is primarily about the rights that are given to parents and students regarding student educational records, it also speaks to the level of confidentiality that should exist for the IEP within a school building as they're often some of the most casually shared educational records for students.

The contents of the IEP should remain with the IEP team alone to the extent that they need that information as stakeholders of that student. In the past I've directed faculties not to share the identity of or exceptionalities of students whom a teacher colleague doesn't serve. It is very easy for gossip to spread and something as confidential as whether a student has a disability or not is not information that should be useful to everyone in the school building let alone to every adult. I also have directed them to store their accommodations in a secure place. As the primary aspect of the IEP that all teachers are responsible for, the accommodations should be kept securely so that they can be reviewed or accessed when needed. Each school building does documentation somewhat differently, but as a baseline particularly as it concerns instructors who aren't the case manager, it is a good practice to address privacy as it concerns the IEP in the following ways:

- Keep all physical IEPs in a secure environment (usually in a locked cabinet) if they need to be printed at all.
- Ask all instructors to secure their copy of student accommodations
- Do not share the IEP or accommodations with individuals that aren't a part of the IEP team
- Do not print and share full IEP only requested sections or allow the team member requesting them to view it virtually or visit the secure cabinet where the IEP in full is stored
- Instruct team members not to discuss the IEP or its contents with students in public like aloud during instruction, but instead taking that student aside if there's something that needs to be expressed privately
- Do not leave IEPs out, but return them to the secure environment when you aren't using them
- If a parent asks for a copy of the IEP provide it with a secure sharing method
- Ask for a received receipt when providing accommodations to service providers and other teachers

These are some things that you can think about when it comes to the level of privacy that is required in special education particularly as it is required by law to make sure that all parties are appropriately protected. An attention to privacy and as it concerns the rights of the student, parents, and the IEP can be some of the most meaningful practices a special educator can make as it pertains to building a relationship with parents and stakeholders. It is very common to have one teacher learn about a student with a disability's IEP when they aren't a part of the IEP team. Consequently, that teacher might discriminate against that student or because the culture around privacy in the school is so casual, students may find out and treat that student with a disability differently. Under these circumstances it would be quite natural for a student to feel defeated and embarrassed about who they are or how they perform. Not only does this impact the growth and learning of the student, but it can make it back to the parent who may rightfully request some type of corrective action.

The level of understanding that you need to have of special education related law isn't very deep, however it is incredibly important that you study the norms and practices around special education (many of which I've shared in this chapter) and learn to incorporate them into your working life so that you can protect your students and yourself. All of these practices don't have legal mandates (and I am not a lawyer so none of this should be construed as legal advice), however they all can have legal implications if you are outwardly defiant of them because they're all related to compliance. If the culture around your building doesn't require gen ed teacher to provide accommodations it is very easy for a parent to pick up on that when their child's grades are falling due to poor implementation of the IEP because teachers were never given a copy of the IEP accommodations and directed to provide them during instruction. An angry parent can mean abrasive emails, drop ins, and meetings, but it can also mean lawyers.

A good special educator doesn't need to be an attorney to know what to do as it relates to good special education practices. There are more applicable laws to special education (the above were the primary ones) and more cases happen every year in which schools and systems are being held to account for their potentially harmful special education practices. However, it is very easy to stay out of the line of fire. It is very easy from a compliance and legal perspective to maintain a great track record in special education. Special educators just need to have a knowledge base, be receptive to instruction, and always be looking to validate and revalidate their practices.

Chapter 6: The IEP

So far in this survival guide we've reviewed the definition of special education, what a service provider is, how to collaborate, advocacy, as well as certain legal aspects of the profession. Now, we're going to be diving into the nitty gritty for most people, the IEP. Most special educators spend a large portion of their thoughts in this work contemplating, planning, and fretting over the IEP. In fact, it would stand to reason that in your survival guide, this will be the section that you spend the most time reviewing and rereading. The IEP is the foundational document and record the determines the services of a student with a disability. It is incredibly important to special education not merely as a compliance vehicle, but as the story of that student with a disability.

Telling the story of the student with a disability is incredibly useful and impactful to their educational outcomes. A well written IEP is like a treasure map that leads educators directly to the most meaningful practices and programming to help a student with a disability achieve at their highest level. Conversely, a poorly written IEP can have educators chasing rainbows and red herrings until they call it quits and start the IEP again from scratch. In this chapter you'll notice that a well written IEP isn't about filling out all of the sections, and a poorly written IEP isn't about lacking parent participation or having the IEP team agree on services. I've seen hundreds of IEPs and in addition to discussing the core components of the IEP in this chapter we'll be reviewing how to write an IEP well because a poorly written IEP can set a student back months to years. However, writing IEPs can be easy and even fun (at least to me). I will be sharing some strategies that make constructing an IEP straight forward and accessible.

Now before we get into the specific components and strategies related to writing a good IEP, we need to discuss your mindset around IEPs. IEPs can be exhausting, time consuming and challenging. However, the best thing for a special educator to do here is to acknowledge and accept these realities as a natural part of their work. If we as educators attempt to make IEPs not exhausting, or time consuming, or challenging we start to overstep the level of attention and efficacy it takes to write an IEP well. As a result, students will continuously be underserved.

Here are some beliefs and practices that good special education departments use to support the creation of the IEP.

- Use a birthday month schedule for annual review due dates (Summer Birthdays are in May, August generally in September)
- Schedule the IEP a month in advanced
- Have the IEP completely written two weeks in advance of the IEP meeting
- Hold amendment IEP meetings as a regular process to validate or modify services, or to address parental concerns

- Support the IEP team in making the best educational decision for student services instead of prescribing them before the team meets

All of these strategies aren't completely intuitive, but they are important practices so that your IEPs are completed in an efficacious manner. In this chapter we will be unpacking each major part of the IEP, and through that process you'll understand more about why these practices are some you'd want to consider adopting.

Below you will find the 10 major parts of the IEP. We will be discussing what these portions of the IEP are and how they're utilized, but also how to fill them out best and what a special educator should be thinking about when completing them.

Components of the IEP

- Demographics
- Present levels of performance
- Services
- Accommodations
- Transition Plans
- BIP
- Goals and Objectives
- Parent Input
- Special Factors
- Notes

Demographics

The demographics section of the IEP is usually the first part of the IEP that you will see. Although you may see this page of the IEP represented in a variety of different ways depending on what state or school system you work in, the demographics page generally includes the student's name and address, their current enrollment and service school, the date of the IEP and most recent evaluation, the student's grade and age, the name/s of the parent or guardian, and the name eligibility category through which the student is eligible for services as a student with a disability. Below are the most common eligibilities that you will see in most states.

- Autism
- Deafblind
- Deaf/Hard of Hearing (D/HH)
- Emotional & Behavioral Disorder
- Intellectual Disabilities
- Orthopedic Impairment
- Other Health Impairment
- Significant Developmental Delay
- Specific Learning Disability
- Speech-Language Impairment
- Traumatic Brain Injury
- Visual Impairment & Blindness

On the demographics page you will likely see these categories abbreviated. To learn more about these categories visit your state's department of education website.

The demographics page is a very important resource for special educators because it gives a lot of information. When it comes to who your student is and where they came from the demographics page is most likely the first thing that you're going to review. Often special educators will need to do research on a student, especially if that student is new or has been hopping from multiple service school locations as they've matriculated. By reviewing it, you'll find right away the name and contact information for old schools, parents and guardians, and even the previous case managers names. It can tell you at a glance, where you need to go and what you should be thinking about when it comes to a student with a disability.

Luckily, the demographics page of the IEP does not happen to be a section that case managers manually fill out. It is usually auto-populated from a school or district database. However, it is important to review that section of the IEP with parents during the IEP meetings to ensure that the information doesn't need to be updated. Therefore, like all sections of the IEP it is important not to gloss over the demographics page because the information that it presents is important to the student.

Present Levels of Performance

The present levels of performance (PLOP), also known as the present levels of academic achievement and functional performance (PLAAFP), will be the section of the IEP that takes the most time to enter and most likely the most time to present during an IEP meeting. As we review this section of the IEP, you'll learn why this is and must be the case, because if the present levels of performance are the quickest part of the IEP to be completed it may be an indication that something has gone wrong.

The present levels of performance can be broken down into the following sections: Eligibility baseline data, Student baseline achievement data, Strengths and Weaknesses, and a statement of impact of the disability on the student's educational performance. Below you'll find a review of the aforementioned components of an IEP's present levels of performance.

Eligibility Baseline Data/ Evaluations

In the PLOP, the first section should include any of the most recent evaluations that were conducted on the student with a disability to determine their special education eligibility. The assessments provided in this section can include intelligence quotient assessments, emotional behavioral assessments, psychological assessments, academic assessments, or any other test that was used in the student's most recent evaluation (As you become more familiar with these assessments, you'll notice the most common ones noted in this section by name). This section is usually produced directly from the student's most recent full psychological evaluation. In many cases you'll notice that the assessments, the dates the assessments were taken, and their scores are transcribed directly from that document. When doing this as a case manager, it is important however, not only to include the assessments and scores, but to also include the summary of what those scores indicate whether it be high or low performance on any particular indicator or a narrative summary of the measure. The most recent evaluation section is highly important information. Although it may not always reflect a student's current ability especially as the student grows and may be a year or two removed from their last evaluation, it does provide useful clues as to underlying issues or historical data that should inform things that you may notice in the classroom or in the student's achievement. If for some reason the data that should be in this section of the PLOP isn't present or available (as it was lost when the student migrated between education systems), it is a best practice to include any relevant achievement or psychological testing recent or otherwise obtained from outdated evaluations. Since psychological evaluations are to be conducted at least every 3 years according to IDEA, if the student has been in special education more than 4 years and the most recent evaluation is either missing or destroyed it is advisable to include an older evaluation in this section to ensure that type of relevant information isn't overlooked.

One thing to understand about this section and by extension any section of an IEP is the importance of retrieving missing data. I've observed plenty of IEPs where if the information wasn't present in the last IEP it is forgone in the subsequent IEPs until the student eventually has a reevaluation. This is not a good practice. If for some reason information is missing, it is the case managers job to request or research where that information is located. Oftentimes, this may mean contacting your system's central office for paperwork assistance, asking a parent, or calling a previous school system to request the records that are missing from the IEP. This section of the PLOP is notoriously challenging particularly for being either vacant or so unnecessarily jargon ladened with specific assessment terms and scoring metrics that it is incomprehensible. In the former case, the best thing for case managers to do is to make sure that some information gets into this section.

It is inappropriate to leave this (or any section of the IEP) blank because it does impact the IEP team's ability to make effective decisions or even advise the parent. For instance, if a student has a recorded IQ at the time of the last evaluation that was unusually low, it may indicate that the student has significant processing issues. Yet, these same processing issues may not be evident or even manifest as such in a classroom setting. The student may get angry when they have trouble processing or start talking. Consequently, that student may receive accommodations for behavior rather than the processing accommodations that their most recent evaluations indicate that they need.

Sometimes, depending on the system you're in and the technology they use, this section of the IEP may also include achievement data on standardized tests. Often that too can be auto-filled from within your system's database. If it is not present, there or at all, the most recent evaluations can be a good place to note how students have scored in their most recent statewide assessments.

Ex: Student A scored a 435 on the State Reading assessment which indicates "meeting expectations" – 4/18/2024.

Strengths and Weaknesses

Strengths and weaknesses tend to be the part of the PLOP that gets the most attention. It is generally easier to write and at this juncture of the IEP meeting you may tend to have more participation from both parents and teachers. As the name suggests, this is the section of the IEP where all of the students' academic, functional, and behavior strengths and weaknesses should be noted. Depending upon the structure of your IEP software, this section could be broken down a number of different ways like by academic subject areas or by each of these three main areas of strengths and weaknesses. Below we'll review each category:

Academic

Academic strengths and weaknesses tend to be the easiest section of writing the IEP. This category is about providing a detailed review of the student's ability in their academic subjects. This could include information about their abilities in English, writing, math, science, or social studies. Generally, the academic category is for information related to the core academic subjects. It doesn't generally include how the student functions academically in special classes like music or gym. However, if that information is relevant to the manifestations of their disability, mentioning their functioning in special classes as well can be appropriate.

When writing about the student's strengths and weaknesses in the academic category it is best to approach this through a standards-based lens. The case manager should identify the standards which the student is required to master according to their specific grade level. The strengths and weaknesses should be based upon those standards. For example, if the student is in 5th grade and is required to do long multiplication, but doesn't do so successfully 80% of the time, a strength might come in their ability to construct the math statement while lining up place values and a weakness may come in their ability to use the cross-multiplication steps. Although aligning numbers in place value rows to construct math statements is a 2nd or 3rd grade skill, it is a strength pertaining to their ability to complete their grade level standard.

Additionally, what's of equal important to dictating a student's standards-based strengths and weaknesses is also noting in this section the student's functional level in that subject area. If a student is in 5th grade and qualifies for special education services in reading, but functions independently on the 3rd grade level in reading it needs to be noted in the strengths and weaknesses. This information is important for many things; one of them being the construction of IEP goals (which we will discuss later on in this chapter). Not only should goals be based on weaknesses, but knowing the student's functional level in any subject area will allow the special educator to construct goals that not only help the student meet the grade level standard, but also remediate that student on standards they haven't mastered to better propel them to independence on their grade level. For instance, the student may be functioning independently on the 3rd grade level in reading because of their comprehension. However, if we dig further, it may turn out that his deficit in reading comprehension is related to his exposure to new words which on the 5th grade level are increasingly based in Latin and Greek roots which he doesn't come across in his daily life. This nuance is the difference between writing an IEP goal related to reading texts and answering multiple choice comprehension questions and one based in vocabulary study and acquiring new words with Latin or Greek roots. Understanding a student's functional academic levels means that an assessment of skills has be taken. Beyond telling you what grade level the student is independent, it reveals skills gaps and depending on what those skill gaps are, like comprehension issues related to key details versus word study, they can point you in very different directions.

As a function of writing a meaningful academic strengths and weaknesses section in an IEP it is integral that students have been assessed in the area that you are providing that information. In fact, it is advisable for subject specific academic assessments to be the first thing mentioned in these strengths and weaknesses. It helps set the stage for the narrative that follows which should include specifics about the student's performance in the classroom setting.

Ex: On the Mathematics First placement test taken on 8/22/2023, (student) scored on the 3rd grade level which indicates his overall independent math proficiency.

Functional

The functional section of your student's strengths and weaknesses are generally about the ways in which your student is adapting to the physical and social components of their educational program. This portion of the strengths and weaknesses answers questions related to how the student is navigating the classroom environment, following social norms and rituals, and transitioning between settings. The social aspects of this section at times do blend into speech and communication, a section generally addressed by the speech pathologist. However, like occupational and physical therapy needs (or any other therapy), which fall under the functional category and would make this category necessary to include, the job of the special educator is to speak to the students' individualized needs and current level of functioning. If the student has areas of concern that they don't or didn't originally qualify for in their eligibility it is still appropriate to note them in the PLOP. In this section you might see information that describes their ease or difficulty using a pencil or getting into and out of a school desk. Functional abilities are very important because they generally cater to the physical aspects of disability that academic achievement doesn't capture. Even if students don't have or qualify for services that are based upon their functional abilities, small things like a student's height or weight can impact their ability to interact with their educational environments without difficulty, not to mention motor control issues, or vision and hearing deficits. Potentially, that difficulty can burden academic performance. You may not see functional strengths and weaknesses noted on every IEP, but they are an important part to include particularly when concerns are present.

Behavior

Like the Functional strengths and weaknesses behavior is generally only necessary to include if the student qualifies for services for a behavior related disability or if they have behavior concerns. It is usually quite obvious what behavioral issues a student needs to have noted in their IEP, but to make sure that they are written appropriately there are 2 things that a special educator should keep in mind: 1) Include the strengths, 2) the antecedent of the behavior.

One of the things that many IEPs tend to miss (particularly with students who have significant maladaptive behaviors) is to include the student's behavioral strengths. If this aspect of their behavior is neglected it can impact the team's ability to leverage important strengths in resolving the negative behaviors that they're displaying. Strengths can come in the form of positive relationships they have, times during the day in which they follow directions well, or in activities that they particularly enjoy. Practically, it is also very good to help parents and other stakeholders feel that you aren't being biased in your assessment of their child's behaviors.

Secondly, the intention of any part of the PLOP is to identify needs, but unlike other parts of the PLOP, the behavior section must have a directly stated antecedent. The antecedent of the behavior is what caused the behavior to occur or what was the stimulus that directly preceded the behavior in question. When writing other areas of the PLOP like academic strengths and weaknesses the antecedent is implied. "The student scores an average of 80% on algebra assessments," may be one line of text as a strength, but the antecedent of that strength is that the student was given grade level math instruction and then given an assessment by their teacher at the end of the week. With behavior the antecedent of the behavior cannot be implied. If a student is breaking all of their pencils during independent practice as a behavior, one cannot assume that the behavior is related to the academic subject, the instructor, or the environment. It can be a combination of all of these stimuli or none of them. This is why it is highly important that prior to the IEP meeting, the case manager has conducted some type of assessment or review to determine when and why the behaviors the student is exhibiting are happening. It can at times be quite obvious why they're occurring, however, at times you need to observe the student, question the adult in the environment when it occurs, and conduct an assessment like an Antecedent/ Behavior/ Consequence (ABC) assessment to determine the cause of the student's behavior. If the behavior is being displayed only at certain times or with a certain teacher, ask the teacher to take notes when it occurs and to explain when and why they believe the behavior is occurring.

Here is an example of a line from a behavior section in the PLOP that doesn't have an antecedent:

"Timmy kicks his feet in math class and makes objects fall from his and other students' desks."

Now with an antecedent:

"Timmy has displayed anxiety around small group time because he has to show his individual knowledge. As the time comes to transition to that class activity, he regularly will start kicking his desk or those around him from his chair to distract himself causing objects to fall from his and other students' desks."

In the examples above you may notice that the behavior hasn't changed, it is still kicking the desk. However, when we include an antecedent, we learn more information about why Timmy is doing the behavior. What the first example doesn't do is allow the IEP team to determine an effective accommodation or solution for the behavior because there is no why. A special educator can write the behavior section of the PLOP to be ten pages long, but if the antecedent isn't present, you cannot suggest or provide effective accommodations or programming to resolve the behavior. Moreover, even if a general accommodation does eliminate the behavior, if you don't identify the antecedent the student will likely create a different behavior to serve the need that wasn't met.

Additionally, it is highly important to be as specific as possible as it concerns when and how often the behavior is taking place. The case manager must indicate, as a best practice, when and where the behavior is occurring during the day. That can be the difference between determining that the antecedent is related to the environment or time of day rather than some maladaptive coping behavior on the student's part. Most negative behaviors are essentially coping mechanisms and it is the job of the IEP team to accommodate the fundamental need. However, if the behavior section isn't specific and it is assumed that the student does the behavior at all times when the behavior is only related to a specific class or even one teacher's seating arrangement, the team may end up creating programming and accommodations that create unnecessary barriers to the student's independent academic functioning.

When the PLOP is not specific, student behaviors like teasing a peer can be seen as generally maladaptive behaviors rather than situational. The teasing could be related to a crush that sits close to the student or someone they don't like. The team may then create an accommodation that requires the student to be seated separately at all times, and as a result the student then misses out on times when they can learn and engage appropriately with their peers during instruction in every class setting rather than just the one in which the behavior actually occurs.

In general, when it comes to the behavior section of the PLOP it is very important that it is completed with care. Particularly for students who qualify for service because of behavior functioning, parents can become very scared of what is inevitably going to be written in this section. They may become defensive especially if they know their child is out of control, they don't have the solution, and the special educator is not providing any real answers. The best way to complete the behavior section of the PLOP is to be direct and balanced while explaining the behavior and why it is occurring as specifically as possible.

The Impact Statement

Among all of the sections of the PLOP the impact statement has the most continuity between various versions of the IEP. It should always be present regardless of the student's current functioning. The impact statement is essentially a summary of the ways in which the student's disability impacts their ability to function educationally and thereby necessitating the provision of special education services. It is a short statement, usually 3 sentences or less, but it can be highly impactful. The impact statement should be a compact summarization of the things that were covered in the PLOP as it's related to that student's specific diagnosis or disability. This statement is usually found directly after the present levels of performance.

It generally can be described as having three parts if you want to be as clear as possible:

1) State the disability

2) Explain how that disability manifests or impacts the student's education

3) Qualifying service statement.

The qualifying service statement only restates the need of the student to receive special education services based upon the manifestations of the student's disability as explained in the first 2 parts of the statement. (From state to state/ district to district you may find that some case managers leave off the third part as the statement is technically complete without it, but the statement is most effective with the final part). Below you'll find an example of a good impact statement for you to use as a case manager in your PLOP.

"Jada holds a diagnosis of dyslexia and depressive disorder. Her disability keeps her from reading at a rate that is comparable to grade level expectations and impacts her ability to independently acquire information in all subject areas. Therefore, Jada requires special education services to gain access to the general curriculum."

*Also, please note that any medications or medical specifications the student receives related to the student's disability are often noted in this section. It is highly important to include those specifications. (Please see your special education school leadership for guidance).

Writing in Narrative Form

The final and most important thing that every special educator needs to remember when writing the PLOP is to write the PLOP in narrative form. The PLOP should not read as a research data log. The PLOP should read like a business article. It should not read as a technical manual. The PLOP needs to read as a narrative. You may have noticed above that when I gave examples of writing in the various sections of the PLOP that I wrote in very much a narrative form (ex: *The student* **does this when** *in* **this** *setting* **because** *of* **this which implies that** *and would* **therefore** *benefit* **from this or that**). The reason I gave you examples in this form is because of the hundreds of IEPs I've seen over the years a good portion (healthy portion) of them are completely unintelligible because the case manager who wrote them didn't write in narrative form. Writing in narrative form makes the PLOP comprehensive, removes the barrier of jargon, and makes the information easily applicable. The psychologist in the IEP initial evaluation process actually lays the groundwork for this practice. After every evaluation, which can be heavy with jargon and other scientific terms and metrics, they provide a clear narrative summary of the evaluation with clear recommendations. It is completely unacceptable that when a psychologist can provide a clear, easy to read narrative of their clinical determinations that a case manager can then take the IEP and fill it with sentence fragments, bullet points, acronyms, and metrics such that none aside from themselves can understand it fully. The PLOP should always be in narrative form. Below is an additional example of what you want to avoid and what you want to do.

To Avoid when filling out your PLOP:

"Charlie scored a 482.1 on Fanci-Brigum Assessment. On the MFAB battery: 45-78; 67;88. Popo & Young Assessment: 89.2 intermediate."

Proper Narrative Form:

"Charlie took the Fani-Brigum Assessment that measures behavioral intelligence on April 7, 2022. He scored a 482.1 which falls in the developing range. Strengths on the assessment were noted in processing and redirection. Weaknesses on the assessment were noted in impulsivity."

Services

In this section we'll be covering special education services. Special education services are more than just the special education classroom (which most lay people tend to think special education services are). Special education services are essentially any time the student is being instructed by someone other than a general education teacher. It can be therapy, classes, or even counseling. In this section we will be reviewing the types of services that special education students can receive; however, we will be spending the majority of this section focusing on the logic and reasoning under which the case manager should be operating when it is time to suggest services. The reason why we'll be structuring this section in this way (and this is important to remember) is because special education services are not determined by the case manager, they are determined by the IEP team. It is very common to believe because case managers are often given the responsibility of suggesting services or even placing students in classes that they make that decision alone, but they do not. IEP services are determined and agreed upon by the entire IEP team without exception.

The services section is typically broken down into 4 distinct sections: service, setting, frequency of service, and providers. We'll review each of these sections describing what special educators should be looking for in these sections. For a full description of every service type and the full range of services that can be provided to a student with a disability please visit your state's department of education web page.

Part 1: Services

Below you will find a list of the most common services in special education and a brief description of their most commonly held definitions.

❖ **Consultative**: When a student with a disability doesn't require routine services that an educator would provide on or near a daily basis. "Consult" services can be provided to the student in which their case manager may confer or conference with that student on a weekly or monthly basis to review their current performance.

❖ **Therapy**: Therapy can be a number of different services provided by any therapist assigned to work with the student most commonly Speech, Occupational, and Physical.

❖ **Academic Instruction***: Instruction isn't a service, but represents the times in which students are receiving special education services during an instructional period. IEP instruction will typically be listed as the subject on that student's academic schedule for which the student is receiving service. (Ex: Math, Reading, Physics, Biology, Social Student, etc.)

- ❖ **Counseling**: Counseling can be listed on an IEP as a service for times the student is schedule to be seen by a counselor
- ❖ **Supportive Services:** Supportive instruction describes a collection of services that are provided to a student with a disability by someone other than a certified special educator or general educator that may include therapists, counselors, but are also provided by para-professionals, job coaches, and other professionals.

Hybrid Terms: You may notice that there are few terms that describe both services and settings. Some districts use these terms interchangeably to describe services rendered to students. Understand that these are delivery models and therefore services, but they also connote a setting so you will find them here and again in the settings section.

- **Small Group** – When a student with a disability is served by a special educator outside of the general education setting in a group that is less than the size of an average class.
- **Collaborative** – A service in which a student is instructed by both a general education teacher and a special education teacher at the same time for less than a full instructional segment. This service is conducted in the general education setting.
- **Co-Taught** – A service in which a student is instructed by both a general education teacher and

a special educator at the same time for a full instructional segment. This service is conducted in the general education setting.

Part 2 & 3: Setting and Frequency

Setting

Below you will find a list of the most common settings in which special education services can take place and a brief description of each. Please, bear in mind that when you see the setting on an IEP it doesn't always correspond to what is happening in the real world in the most direct manner. In these special cases the services that the student is being provided may fit within two categories. One example would be if a hospital/homebound program provided a co-teaching environment to students in which there is a special education and general education teacher teaching together in that setting. In these cases, you have to read the IEP and the notes in their entirety to get a full picture of the manner in which a student is or was being served. Additionally, when you see the special education and general education settings understand that depending on what IEP software is being used, or what state or district you're in, these terms may be used in addition to or in lieu of other setting terms like small group or collaborative as students receive small group instruction in the special education setting and collaborative instruction in the general education setting.

- **General Education** – A class setting in which a student with a disability is instructed alongside students without disabilities.

- **Special Education** – A class setting in which students with disability are not served alongside their peers without disabilities
- **Hospital/ Homebound** – A program setting in which a student's educational program is supplemented in a hospital or home and is provided to students to ensure continuity between their regular class program when their disability makes them unable to attend school on a regular basis.
- **Residential** – this is a placement of a child with a disability in a public or private residential program or facility to provide the necessary services required by the student's IEP
- **Home-based** – Is a service in which the student with a disability is provided direct service at their home by a special educator. Unlike hospital/ homebound this service is provided typically on a short-term basis and isn't necessarily provided due to the nature of a medical diagnosis.
- **Separate Day School*** - This is a service in which the student is provided instruction and service by a special educator in a program and or school other than the one in which they are placed or enrolled based upon the agreement of the IEP team. (On an IEP this service may not say "Separate Day School", but rather be named in accordance with the title of the actual program where they're being serviced.)

Frequency of Service

The frequency in which a student with a disability is served is of high importance to the fidelity of their educational program. Ultimately, frequency is determined by hours per unit of time.

Ex: Math – 5 hr/wk

        Math- 1 hour segment, 5 times/week

        Math – 60 min/day 5 times per week

You may notice that hours are written differently in different systems, but they should all correspond to something that is easily identified on a student's academic schedule. In terms of process, the only service that has a recommended or prescribed number of hours or minutes are consultative services. Consultative services are provided to students who generally don't require the daily services or interventions provided by an IEP. Consultative services may look like a 1-hour conversation between the student and the student's case manager once a month (ex: Consultative – 1 hr/mo; Consultative – 15 min/wk). For all other services provided by the IEP it is up to the IEP team and the service providers on that team to determine the recommended number of hours the student's required to meet that student's educational needs.

Bear in mind, the hours that a student is assigned is highly important to their success. Overserving, giving the student more hours than they reasonably need, or underserving, giving the student fewer hours than they reasonably need, can have a dramatic effect the student's achievement. Overserving a student can diminish that student's rate of academic growth. Being overserved will cause them to miss out on key moments and lessons that are taking place in school environments that they would have been present for if they weren't receiving special education services at that time. Being underserved can seriously exacerbate the effects of the student's disability on their academic achievement that should have otherwise been mitigated. In either case, the student is not in their least restrictive environment. Determining the number of hours is a very difficult skill to master (which is why in many schools the number of service hours is prescribed prior to the IEP meeting. which is also why schools have a tendency to overserve students rather than underserve them) so determining what is the least restrictive is best decided upon by the entire IEP team rather than a singular special educator.

Determining how many hours of service or the frequency of service, and moreover what is a more or less restrictive service (services in the general education setting being a less restrictive environment than those in the special education setting) is actually far less difficult as the student matriculates. High school students, because they have specific learning criteria through which they earn credits and eventually a diploma (which is recognized by the state), require a more linear path to their academic instruction based special education services. To meet that requirement, most high schools utilize co-teaching services far more than other types of special education academic services. Often in middle school and particularly in elementary school determining the frequency of services is more flexible and more impactful. In elementary school, unlike high school, everything the student learns is designed to build upon previously learned knowledge. Any time an IEP team determines that a student will not be in the general education setting for services, that student may be missing out on key, foundational information that may not be revisited in the same manner again. It can be an important math principle regarding estimation or a science principle about soil erosion. Additionally, scheduling in elementary schools can be more difficult because subjects tend to blur into one another on an academic schedule rather than having as uniform timeslots as in high school.

Below you'll find a graph explaining the differences between a more and less restrictive environment and service frequency for special education.

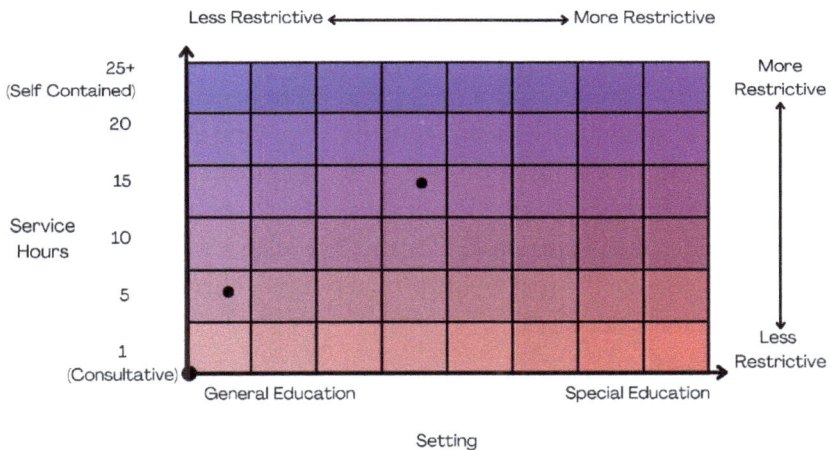

Service Chart for Identifying and Comparing the Least Restrictive Environment

Ultimately what the chart communicates is that the special education setting is more restrictive than the general education setting, and more service hours is more restrictive than fewer hours. For a student to be serviced entirely in the general education settings (in the case that the student only has collaborative services or to a further degree is consultative) is to say that all of that student's education needs can be met in that environment with tools and resources that can be provided in that environment. Conversely, for a student to be serviced entirely in the special education setting is to say that the student's education needs cannot be met in the general education setting at all and that the special education instruction will replace the instruction typically given in the general education setting. The difference between these two poles of the spectrum of service (both the setting and the frequency of service) will determine what type of instruction is given, what resources the student will have access to, and ultimately the academic trajectory of that student. I've seen students in the special ed setting who are leaps and bounds performing at higher levels than general education students, but are served there because that's what they're used to. I've seen students in general education setting who can barely function due to the manifestations of their disability, because that service was determined by someone outside of the current IEP team. I've seen a lot of students who receive the just right fit of services. This is a highly important decision.

Part 4: Service Provider

The service provider is the person who is responsible for providing the service to the student. This person is usually identified last in the service section of the IEP. Some common service providers include: Special Educator, Para-Professional, Counselor, Speech Therapist, Occupational Therapist, and Physical Therapist. Who serves a student is a decision that can be implied by default by which professional under a certain program or title works in a particular school, but is ultimately a decision made by the IEP team as in some cases multiple professionals can be qualified to provide different service types to students with disabilities. To get a full review of which professionals can provide which services consult your state's Department of Education website. Another key understanding in regards to service providers is that on the IEP the service provider is not listed in the services section by name, but rather title. The purpose of this regulation is to ensure that the student can receive services from any professional with that title and qualifications. Naming a service provider in this section would make them bound to that service and would cause that student's IEP to be out of compliance if for whatever reason that service provider could no longer provide that service (as would be the case if the student moved to a different school) or if they were no longer employed by that school system.

Accommodations

The accommodations section of the IEP is the place in which the unique measures designed to help the student gain access to the curriculum are provided. This section of the IEP should directly reflect the present levels of performance as the measures provided in this section should be designed to mitigate the manifestations of a student's disability so that they can gain access to the curriculum. For instance, if the present levels indicate that the student has trouble manipulating a pencil and requires occupational therapy, a number of accommodations could be useful in supporting that student's growth including: access to pencil grips, wide lined paper for writing, graph paper for math, and extended time for written responses. The above example demonstrates that any one manifestation can benefit from or even necessitate multiple accommodations. It is up to the IEP team to be inventive and creative when determining which accommodations are provided to a student. Some of the questions that case managers and the IEP team itself needs to ask when determining accommodations are "What is going to be asked of the student academically?" and "What is going to help the student reach their academic and IEP goals?".

When providing these accommodations to students the IEP team considers the 4 primary types of accommodations: **Presentation** (instructional formats and how information is presented to the student, like larger print), **Response** (How the student is allowed to provide responses to the assignments or instruction, like allowing oral responses for quick assignments), **Setting** (Where the student is provided instruction, like small group instruction as needed), and **Scheduling** (when instructional activities take place, like shorter testing sessions over multiple days). All accommodations should fall into one of these 4 categories.

There are accommodations that are common that every student seems to get. I will list those common accommodations below. However, when it comes to the fidelity of an IEP, the team has to think beyond what they've done in the past and what is easy to implement. Not only is this important so that the student gets the "right fit" accommodation, but also because if the team is lazy about deciding which accommodations to provide it will likely be lazy about implementation. Oftentimes, when students are prescribed general or basic accommodations in their IEP, I will find that the student doesn't receive those accommodations regularly, they aren't used to them, they don't know about them, and educators don't know when to provide them in a real environment. Even if they get those accommodations at critical times, like test exam accommodations, because the student is not used to using them 9 times out of 10 the student will either refuse or not use the accommodation during the assessment. This is an observation that is consistent in every special education environment that I've been in. When the accommodation seems to be overly generic (meaning we see the same ones on every IEP) they may not be being integrated into the student's educational program effectively. Of course, some students may only require those most common accommodations, but if the special educator is not providing the same level of attention to general accommodations like checks for understanding that they do to highly specific accommodations like daily behavior contract check-ins they won't be implemented with fidelity.

Below are some of the most commonly provided accommodations:

- Checks for understanding
- Extended time for responses
- Oral Reading of test questions
- Preferential seating
- Frequent Monitored Breaks
- Reduced assignments
- Extended time for Test and Exams

Important for special educators to be aware of when providing accommodations is the difference between an accommodation and a modification. Modifications differ from accommodations in that they don't merely change the method through which students are gaining access to their educations, modifications change the academic objective. Quite in the same way that in gifted learning programs the educational goals for students are more rigorous than in a regular classroom, a modification in special education is designed to meet a student on their instructional level. A modification for students with disabilities in the classroom may look like having one learning objective (ex: Summaries in reading) rather than 2 or 3 (ex: inference and key details in reading). It could also mean assigning only certain problems to a student during an assessment rather than all of the problems that they may receive in their general classroom. For the special educator it is highly important that they understand the difference and don't provide accommodations when they need to provide a modification and don't provide a modification when they mean to provide an accommodation.

There are students who, because of the severity of their disability, require some or all of their work to be modified (modified compared to the learning standards of the general education population). The adaptive curriculum is a modified curriculum provided to students with moderate to severe disabilities who as a result cannot meet the state's general standards for learning. However, as this would imply, modifications are more restrictive, and all students don't require them. With LRE in mind, modifications for higher functioning students with disabilities should be viewed as short term. Their purpose in most cases should be to reduce the load on the student as their specific deficit is addressed or improved. Therefore, a review of whether or not the student should be receiving a modification should be had at every IEP meeting on some level if one is being proposed. Furthermore, the special educator needs to be the expert in this regard. Some or most of the other members of the IEP team may not know the difference between a modification and an accommodation and the special educator must provide expert advice. When providing accommodations or modifications, which will appear in the same section of the IEP, the team needs to consider the present levels, the impact of the disability on the student, the student's educational trajectory, and the least restrictive environment as the key determining factors of how they are provided.

Transition Plans

Transition plans are a portion of the IEP that is designed to provide students with the roadmap of how they enter the community after graduation from high school. When constructing a transition plan, which takes several years to complete, the case manager is meeting with the student to determine their progress, discussing and assessing their strengths/weaknesses and aspirations, and helping to provide them with resources that will lead them to the post-secondary outcomes they're looking for. There are a lot of stakeholders in this process which are integral to making sure it is completed with fidelity like the parent, student, and a transition specialist (who in many systems actually leads this process). The primary components of the transition plan include post-secondary education/ training, employment, and independent living. In most states, the transition plan should be started by the time the student turns 16, but to gain further understanding about this process in your state it is best to consult your state's department of education website.

Most IEPs won't contain a transition plan, however, when you do interact with them and the entire transition process it is important to be as transparent and open as possible with the student and their families. At the point in a student's educational career that they actually need a transition plan, they should already be attending every IEP meeting as a critical team member. So, as the transition plan is discussed and cultivated, the student needs to be the driving force of its creation and needs to be a part of the entire process. Having worked with students with IEPs in high school, there are so many students that I've seen with transition plans that were poorly orchestrated. Either they didn't include the necessary career and aptitude assessments to guide the student toward meaningful career options or the student was in complete misalignment with what the transition plan communicated. Students often didn't want to go to college or the armed forces, those things were merely options for them, and the actual pathway which they desired to pursue post high school was in no way present in their plan. Of course, this can occur year to year as students change their minds about their interests and what they want to pursue. However, it often happens when you have an unhealthy power dynamic with the student. Particularly as students will most likely graduate from high school as adults, it is incredibly important that students know that the transition plan is for them (to some students it's the most meaningful part of the IEP). They shouldn't feel like they need to give responses to their case manager or transition specialist that are "what they want to hear". I've found that often students do this because they don't have honest relationships with their case manager to the extent that they believe the case manager will provide them honest advice and support their desires as an advocate to their parents or any other member of the IEP team. The best approach for these students is to have an attitude of "What do you want?", "Why do you want it?", "Is this sustainable?", and "How can we reasonably get you there?"

Behavior Intervention Plans

The behavior intervention plan (BIP) is a plan for behavior typically given to students who have emotional behavior disorders, but are available to all students who require additional behavior programming. The components of a behavior intervention plan are generally very simple in that they reflect other parts of the IEP. There is an explanation of the behavior, a description of the function of that behavior, a description of the replacement behavior, strategies and techniques for teaching the replacement behavior and/or reinforcing its usage, and some type of data collection measure. An example of the structure of a BIP could be similar to the following: Sara leaves the room without asking: She leaves to room usually to use the bathroom or when she sees a teacher she likes outside of the room: Sara will raise her had to request permission to leave the room each time in 5 out of 5 trails: Supports include, direct instruction; cue cards; positive reinforcement; anchor charts in classroom; preferential seating: Data will be collected weekly 5 of 5 trails.

All BIPs should be generated first through a functional behavior assessment (FBA). This is an assessment that is conducted by a special education case manager or behavior specialist to determine why behaviors are occurring once behavior issues have been brought to their attention. This assessment isn't always a part of the IEP document and is a precursor to the BIP. Most students will also not require a behavior intervention plan.

Some special educators rarely write BIPs, depending on where they specialize their work, however, there are two things in particular that can make or break the implementation of a BIP whether you wrote it yourself or are just implementing the BIP a previous case manager wrote. They are follow-through and being specific.

Out of the many, many BIPs I've read, the ones that are written the most correctly come from behavior intervention specialists whose role it is to write effective plans. There are many others that are written by case managers/special educators. Of those, many end up kneecapping the student's entire educational program because they're written with such an extreme lack of thoughtfulness and detail. Below is an example of one of these BIPs and where they tend to go wrong.

Ex 1:

Student is off-task every day in class and is disruptive continuously.

The student does this to gain attention and avoid classwork.

The student will stay on task 100% of the time and will respond when asked what the class is doing with a correct statement.

Supports include: direct instruction, behavior contract, allowing natural consequences

Data collection: Daily 100%

Now to a lay person, or just an inexperienced special educator this mock BIP may look just dandy. To an experienced behavior interventionist this is probably amateur hour. Let's break this down. Firstly, "off-task" and "disruptive" are undefined. What does it mean to be off-task in class and disruptive? What actual behaviors will the teacher observe? If a student is running around the class in history, they're most likely behaving disruptively. If the same student is running around the class in gym class, they're most likely doing the right thing. You have to be specific and say what observable behaviors the student has manifested. Secondly, the replacement behavior statement is unreasonable. 100% compliance isn't even a reasonable request for a student without a behavior disability. No student is on-task 100% of the time. Furthermore, the statement "respond when asked what the class is doing with a correct statement" isn't a good measure (or any measure) of not being disruptive or being off-task. The student can very literally be bouncing off the walls and give an accurate statement of what the class/they should be doing.

If you will, let's take this a little further and imagine that we've met the student in this example and know them well. We've determined the observable behaviors are pushing other students, cursing at adults and students, and instigating fights by bullying. These behaviors are indeed disruptive. The student very well could also be doing these behaviors for attention or to avoid classwork, however, the BIP as is, is completely inappropriate and insufficient to address the actual behaviors. The BIP might as well have been written for a different student because the strategies and descriptions are completely detached from the manifestations of the student's behaviors. In fact, this BIP could be even dangerous to implement. Allowing natural consequences to occur is a great strategy (in fact they all could be in the right case) when there is a robust behavior management system in place where the student will miss out on positive rewards for exhibiting the behavior of focus, however if the natural consequences of the actual behaviors is fighting and the potential of students or teachers being hurt it is aggressively inappropriate.

Here is how this BIP might be adjusted to better meet the level of efficacy students in special education require:

Ex 2:

Student is off-task every day **as evidenced by putting their head down and whining in class, the whining causes disruptions**.

The student does this to gain attention and avoid classwork.

The student will stay on task **80% of the class period as evidenced by sitting up and following teacher instruction and will respond to redirection for whining within 2 attempts.**

Supports include: direct instruction, behavior contract, allowing natural consequences, **redirection, positive reinforcement, checks for understanding**

Data collection: **Weekly 4/5 trials, Frequency data chart**

In this modified exemplar BIP, not much was changed, but it is already leagues better than it was. I will also point out that the phrase, "as evidenced by" can be a lifesaver particularly if you don't know the best language to describe the behaviors you're tracking.

Unfortunately, the reality is that BIPs often do look like the first example. It is the responsibility of the case manager and all special educators to become comfortable writing BIPs and asking for help with them when needed. They must be comfortable deferring to those with more experience than them to support their construction as well as to write smart goals (which we will discuss in the next section).

Goals and Objectives

Goals and objectives like the Behavior Intervention Plan is something that should be based on the information provided in the present levels of performance directly. The goals and objectives are designed to meet the developmental and academic needs of the student as they are noted as weaknesses in the PLOP. Therefore, if behavior, math, and science were noted as weaknesses in PLOP there should be a corresponding goal for each area identified located in this section of the IEP. When writing a goal for an IEP the acronym SMART is often used to describe how a goal should be generated with the highest level of fidelity. SMART in the context of education stands for specific, measurable, achievable, relevant, and time-bound. SMART goals, first coined by George T. Dorn in 1981, provide the necessary framework to ensure that the goals generated for students with disabilities are capable of successfully driving their improvement. Below you will find an example of a smart goal:

Stella will be able to calculate two-digit addition equations using learned mathematical strategies with a pencil and paper by the end of the academic year with 85% accuracy.

The goal above is specific (naming the student and what she'll be able to do), measurable (she must answer the equations with 85% accuracy, achievable (something that is determined based upon recommendations from the student's instructors), relevant (determined by the student's age and grade; this may be a perfect goal for a 2nd grade student according to that curriculum), and time-bound (she must complete this goal by the end of the academic year. This format for constructing goals in the IEP should be applied to all areas of weakness in the same manner regardless of whether they are for academic needs, communication, therapy, developmental, etc.

One thing that many inexperienced special educators may not be aware of in writing these goals is that you have to not only write smart goals, but also write goals that can address multiple needs. What a special educator should notice about different populations of students is that they write goals slightly differently. Autism classes, moderate, and even severely/profoundly disabled populations of students will likely have multiple developmental, therapy, and academic goals to address both the severity and complexity of their specific needs based upon the characteristics of their disability. High functioning students, students who may receive instruction primarily in the general education setting tend to have fewer areas of need to address through goal setting. However, regardless of how many areas of need must be represented in the goals and objectives section of the IEP, each goal should be written to serve as many needs as possible at once.

Some students with disabilities may come into special education with only one area of need identified (like math or reading) but because of the severity of their disability may have very many skill deficits. Based upon their developmental or grade level expectations these skill deficits can reach into the dozens. Yet, it isn't appropriate to write dozens of IEP goals for one student. So, what should the special educator do? Special educators have to make it their aim to craft goals that are not just Smart, but both efficient and relevant.

Efficient IEP goals are ones designed to meet as many skill deficits as possible. If a student has math deficits which include multiplication calculation, word problem solving, and place value representation, instead of creating three goals (which many novice special educators do) one goal can be made to address each skill deficit. - *Ex: Darwin will solve multiplication word problems by correctly identifying the correct integers to multiply, writing the correct equation, and solving with 90% accuracy by the end of the IEP cycle.* – In this way all of the deficits are addressed (as they are all required to meet this goal) and the special educator doesn't need to produce multiple forms of assessment to probe the student on their mastery. Additionally, when at all possible (which generally it is very possible), evidence of student progress should come naturally from the student's routine classwork. Many students have classes every day where they are assigned work identified in their IEP goals, work that doesn't need to be recreated for the sake of assessment. Another mistake of the novice special educator is not knowing the curriculum well enough to see, in the student's daily work, where they're already practicing the skill in question. If there is a spelling test every single week in a student's class the student doesn't need to be pulled out of class or to the back of the room to complete a spelling probe to collect data for their IEP that addresses the same skill. It is not only unnecessary, but often inappropriate when students with IEPs are already (quite often) inundated with assessments to the extent that they have no time to practice the skills on which they're being assessed.

If I know that the general education teacher is going to provide a student with a math assessment every week to test her skills as a natural component of their class or if the student is in your own class and you know that you're going to assess all of your students on that skill on a regular basis, it is a waste of instructional time to then set aside more time to probe a student on skills that have already been assessed. This can and often does lead to student burnout and disengagement. Assessment should only be approximately 10% of the school week.

When we create goals that encapsulate multiple skills, we create assessments that encapsulate multiple skills. This and pulling naturally occurring evidence of student data creates positive programming that will keep students engaged and motivated. When this isn't done, the IEP and specifically goal setting and the assessment needed to track goals becomes a burden on the student instead of a support.

Furthermore, special educators have to make sure that the goals that are set for students with disabilities are relevant. Every goal should be written with the intention of achieving the student's long-term educational needs and development milestones. Every skill deficit is not relevant to that intention. Having a student with moderate to severe autism learn about the differences between different types of flowers is not a meaningful goal for them to have. Having a second-grade general education collaborative student with a disability have a goal about memorizing the moral lesson in a list of fables when that standard is only relevant for the first half of the year is not a meaningful goal for them to have. Forcing a student to learn dining room etiquette when they have a behavior disability is not a meaningful goal for them to have on their IEP. These goals would be irrelevant. All these skills are amiable, and the student may legitimately not know how to do them, but they're not in service of their academic milestones and developmental needs. There are times in which you may see goals like these in an IEP, if they are related to the transition needs or career related goals of the student, but generally they shouldn't be in an IEP.

When a special educator creates irrelevant goals, they end up wasting the student's instructional time and making their educational program less effective. I've seen many students who week by week fail their probes, lose instructional time due to having to take assessments, and otherwise lose the will to engage in special education as a program because the goals are irrelevant. Often a student failing a probe isn't due to their lack of aptitude, but purely based on the fact that probe or assessment isn't in the curriculum and they never have time to practice it. Many special educators will hand a student a probe at the end of the week and tell the student to complete it because it is an IEP goal, but the standard that probe is based on hasn't been in the curriculum for 3 months, so the student fails and the probe is used as evidence of that student not making progress and then the special educator spends even more instructional time reviewing the probe when it isn't relevant to their disability or their curriculum (My head would be spinning). Another common example of this is in math, when students are given remedial multi-step pencil and paper math calculation goals that they hadn't mastered in elementary school, but are now in middle school where all students are required to use calculators anyway. It may seem to some that giving students really specific obscure goals could benefit them in some way (or be otherwise impressive), but this only harms student outcomes.

When generating relevant goals special educators need to ask themselves these questions:

- Is this goal based on the student's present levels of performance?
- Is this a skill that they will need to have long-term?
- Is this goal based upon a standard in the curriculum?
- Does the student need this skill to matriculate?
- Is this goal based upon a standard that the student will need the entire year?
- Will this goal be relevant next year?

I don't want to suggest that you'll never see a goal that seems very specific or irrelevant. However, when crafting goals for students with disabilities, the special educator has to keep in mind that goals and objectives aren't a measure of their inventiveness, but a measure of what skills are going to be the most useful and productive for the student's education. Every single IEP goal must be relevant.

Parental Input

In the IEP the special educator will find a section where parental input is to be documented. What the special educator may find, in IEP meetings, is that one parent may be highly engaged and interested in their child's education program and other parents don't have any major concerns or questions. Yet, this isn't a concern of the special educator because this input must be noted. This parent input section is of high importance because the parent/guardian is the stakeholder who's understanding of and agreement with all educational decisions is of the most impactful to the student's educational program. Not only do parents have the right to continue or revoke special education services, but their support and facilitation of the IEP makes extraordinary impacts on the outcomes of the student.

One best practice when noting parental input is to send the parent a survey prior to the IEP meeting to identify their concerns, questions, or the updates that they'd like to receive during the IEP meeting. This survey is best delivered along with any explanation of parental rights that need to be provided to the parent/guardian prior to or during the meeting. If the parent hasn't responded prior to the IEP meeting, ask the parent when in attendance questions like: What are your concerns with the student's progress; What questions do you have regarding the IEP or your student's progress; and how do you feel about the team's recommendations (identifying the specific recommendations). Try to ask open-ended questions rather than close-ended questions, and record their responses in the appropriate section.

Special Factors

The special factors section of the IEP is a section of the IEP where the team considers certain aspects of the child's developmental profile that may require individualized consideration within the IEP as they may impact the educational program. These factors include:

- Behavior - If the student's behavior impacts their learning or the learning of others
  - If this special factor has been identified an FBA, behavior intervention plan, or additional positive behavior supports should be considered by the IEP team for inclusion in the IEP.
- Limited English Proficiency
  - If this special factor has been identified, notate in the IEP how this specific factor will be addressed. (Most students to whom this special factor applies will also be enrolled in their school's English Second Language program, and a representative of that program will be a part of the IEP team)
- Blindness or Visual Impairment

- If this special factor has been identified, notate in the IEP how this specific factor will be addressed by the IEP program. (Often but not always visual impairment may be the primary eligibility for the student in question)
- Deaf or Hard of Hearing
  - If this special factor has been identified, notate in the IEP how this specific factor will be addressed by the IEP program. (Often but not always hearing impairments may also be represented in that student's eligibility)
- Assistive Technology
  - When assistive technology is selected as a requirement for the student, notate in the IEP which and in what cases the assistive technology service will be necessary for their educational program.

When selected, considerations and supports for these special factors can be noted in various places in the IEP including the accommodations and notes sections of the IEP. The special factors section of the IEP can often be the shortest section to review during an IEP meeting, however it is important that each option is considered thoroughly. For more information regarding the specific qualifications for considering each category please review your state's department of education website.

Notes

The final part of any IEP will be the notes section. In this section the special educator or designated notetaker will write the minutes for the meeting. There are many ways in which minutes can be taken, but it is important that they are taken chronologically and comprehensively. The notes section can be a one stop shop for service providers and future case managers to learn vital information about the student's educational history and past IEP meetings. In the list below are items that are important to include when providing notes to the IEP. Please note that the list is in order of how these items should generally appear in the meeting notes.

- The type of meeting taking place and the purpose of that meeting
- The date of the meeting
- The meeting members present
- Explanation of the provision of parental rights
- An indication that each section of the IEP was reviewed
- A summary of the strengths and weaknesses identified by the team in the PLOP
- The services that the team identified that student will receive
- Any pertinent input, commentary, questions provided by members of the IEP team not otherwise captured in the PLOP or parent input sections and their resolution
- A statement that the minutes were discussed
- A description of any next steps to be completed after the meeting is adjourned

- A description of any pertinent changes to services or supports
- A statement that the meeting was adjourned

Good notes or minutes can be both a time saver and life saver for IEPs. They can help service providers and case managers navigate pages and pages of documentation quickly, and they can also give much needed context to IEPs whose team decisions are confusing or otherwise poorly executed.

In this chapter we reviewed the components of an IEP. If followed with fidelity your IEPs can become a more comprehensive, implementable blueprint of a student with a disability's educational program. As with other legal aspects of special education this isn't legal advice (please see your state's department of education website for the most accurate specifications for compliance) these are best practices for effective results. Moreover, this is an important distinction because what is legally compliant doesn't always provide the best results. It isn't a legal requirement to write smart goals in an IEP. It isn't a legal requirement to answer why and how when it comes to discussing which services a student receives. However, with this level of consideration the outcomes for the implementation of a student's IEP can be dramatically improved. That is the point of an IEP.

Chapter 7: The Medical

When it comes to working with people with disabilities, the medical aspect of disability is highly important. It is the difference between proper and improper care. It is the difference between healthy students and students who may be put in dire medical situations. However, let me start this chapter out by saying special educators are not medical practitioners. We are not doctors (unless you already happen to be one) so we cannot give proper medical opinions and diagnoses. We are not psychologists (unless you already happen to be one) so we cannot provide psychological treatment or provide diagnoses. However, what the special educator is (which is very important to know) is a person who is the most knowledgeable professional in the subject of disability and their related medical requirements that schools interact with on a daily basis for a specific student. That means for any specific student on your caseload, the special educator is the person that should know that disability best, what school related medical needs that disability entails, and any other related needs that student might require throughout the course of the school day. So special educators have to be informed and aware.

When it comes to the general medical history of your students as it pertains to their disability special educators need to know. When it comes to the manifestations of a student's disability, what accommodations are appropriate for the support of that student with a disability, what medications they take, and how their disability may impact their overall functioning while at school special educators need to know. This isn't merely about making sure that students receive their medications on-time on a daily basis. This is about making sure that every student with a disability has a holistic educational program that is reflective of the full range of needs of their disability with the special educator as the primary means of incorporating that program into a school as an advocate.

In service of incorporating that educational program and in addition to having knowledge of student medical histories, their medications, and accommodations that are best utilized for a student's specific disability, the special educator also needs to be aware of comorbidities. Often students with disabilities have multiple medical conditions and some disabilities often come linked to others. For instance, autism is comorbid with types of epilepsy. Many of my students with autism have also had epilepsy. Most students I've served have never exhibited an episode during the school day, but one student I was serving had a seizure right in the middle of his IEP meeting. Special educators have to be aware of contributing factors like comorbidities not only to know what to do in cases of extreme or unique medical episodes, but also for far less rare medical conditions like asthma. Yet, most importantly special educators need to be aware so that they can ask the right questions. Often parents will not know what is relevant information for the school or a case manager to know. So, if you're aware that a diagnosis of ADHD can be comorbid with diagnoses like obsessive-compulsive disorder, you may ask the question "Does he/she have any other diagnoses that we should be aware of?". This is just a general question which any special educator can use to make sure that students are safer and that the work of special education is being done well.

Now what is far less apparent (and less practiced) to the special educator is becoming aware of not only the physical medical needs of the student, but also the medically relevant psychological needs of the student. When it comes to the proper method of teaching students with autism adaptive behavior analysis is a type of therapy that they may already be receiving. The special educator in charge of their instruction, although not always responsible for the implementation of that therapy, should be aware of it and should be looking to incorporate aspects of it into their teaching instruction. With this, the student will be able to better generalize behavior and learning expectations which will ultimately make them more successful. This is also true of students with emotional behavior disorders. Special educators cannot and should not rely on the behavior management practices that are generalized to all students in their school building. Some general behavior management practices in some buildings involve practices that are inappropriate for all students let alone students with disabilities. I've seen educators chastise, taunt, threaten, and otherwise berate students with emotional behavior disorders just because that is what they would do with a regular student to no effect. As a result, the student is disengaged, defiant, and, on the part of the educator, isn't being provided the behavior management techniques that foster cooperation, engagement, and proactivity.

When these students get out of hand due to educators not attending to the student's psychological needs through appropriate and high-quality instruction (which includes behavior management), many teachers end up settling for compliance rather than engagement; in which a student is well fed and docile rather than engaging appropriately with the curriculum. Instead of using therapeutic techniques in instructional delivery, they're given less work. Instead of providing low-stakes, engaging opportunities for academic success, their participation or lack thereof is ignored by the instructor as long as they're quiet. This is not the proper implementation of an IEP for a student with a disability.

Special educators have to be aware of the psychological needs of a student with a disability. The recommendations that every psychologist provides in their evaluations and therapies aren't a matter of good documentation. These recommendations are the principles through which special educators need to instruct and design student educational programs.

Special educators are not meant to be doctors and therapists. We aren't diagnosing. We aren't prescribing medication. However, special educators need to be experts in their building, ready and willing to integrate meaningful ways to incorporate the medical requirements of students into their daily academic routines. This means knowing medications, diagnoses, the best accommodations for student needs, emergency protocols and plans, and having psychologically relevant instructional practices. Yet, this also (and most importantly) means the special educator is making recommendations to the appropriate stakeholders and asking the right questions.

Chapter 8: Data Collection

   In your survival guide we've mentioned briefly some of the tenets of proper data collection for a special educator and a special education department, however it is important that we spend more time taking a focused look at data collection because, anecdotally, it is the hardest part of special education. Data collection is the one thing that special educators will consistently complain about. Either it's too much or they don't know how to do it. Yet, the reality is data collection should not be that "hard". Of course, it is difficult at times, but most of the difficulty related to data collection is top down; administrators and leaders requesting specific or unnecessary levels of data collection. The average caseload of a special educator is really only about 7 students with a high average of 14. I've experienced caseloads of the low 20s and 30s at certain times and I was still able to make it work. Now, these cases were unusual and were necessary based upon the environment in which I was working, but if a special educator has a caseload of roughly 7 students and is struggling with data collection, something is wrong. Granted, having the proper data collection standards and practices is something that you need to petition your special education and school leadership to modify, however, it is doable. In this chapter, we'll be reviewing how to curate an appropriate data collection system around your instruction and case management. What we're going to be talking about in this chapter is of great importance because students with IEPs generally find the level data collection, and tasks associated with that data collection, to be the main contributors to why they are unfocused, defeated, and worn out by their individualized education programs.

Data Collection Methods

The biggest hurdle to jump when it comes to data collection is just knowing what you don't know about the tools and practices that you can utilize as a special educator in your practice. Below is a list of very common and useful data collection methods to utilize in your practice. Once you've found one that you like, take the time to research it, and identify what type of form or data recording tool you'll use to capture information. Often the structure and layout of the data form can be just as impactful as the practice itself when it comes to reducing the burden of data collection (I've modified a great many forms so that they're easy to use and useful to me).

Data Collection Methods

- Direct Observations – Real Time student observation
- Checklists and Rating Scales – using forms to check of skills and behaviors
- Work Samples – Keeping student products from their class
- Data Reports – Reporting forms and records from virtual assessments and work

- Anecdotal Records – Detailed notes of student behaviors
- Frequency Charts – How often a behavior occurs
- Interval Charts – Record whether a behavior occurs within a set time interval
- Permanent Products – Tangible student generated products used to assess skills like writing samples

All of these methods can be utilized with the aid of physical and virtual forms, online systems, apps, and digital tools. However, it is up to the special educator to determine which tool to use because every goal can be assessed accurately with multiple tools and strategies. The difference in the ease of data collection is often about which tool you've decided to use. Please, take the time to research these strategies to see what medium you can use to apply them; to some special educator's, data collection is hard copies printed every Monday, some spreadsheets with automated calculations, and some apps where all you have to do is click a button. Which or what combination is it for you?

Data Collection Mindset

Now that we've reviewed the primary types of data collection that you will be utilizing in special education, it is important that we talk about your mindset toward data collection, because data collection isn't just about tracking goals. In the chapter of your survival guide on IEPs we discussed the importance of writing IEP goals that are both relevant and efficient. This is the number one thing that supports the effective integration of data collection procedures. If you aren't sure about how to write effective IEP goals please review that chapter. Now, we're going to talk about the second step in that process. This step is about how special educators make sure that data collection measures aren't intrusive, exhausting, and aimless. As mentioned earlier in your survival guide, data collection is one of the primary reasons students are dissatisfied with their educational programs. An excess of probing and assessment leaves them unmotivated, sometimes defiant, and missing out on key instructional time. In order to remedy this reality, in order to make sure that students are benefiting from the process of data collection (rather than it being viewed as a requirement with all the intrinsic value of a statewide test) special educators must make sure that their data collection is rigorous, collaborative, and flexible.

Rigorous Data Collection

First let's start by making one key distinction about rigorous data collection; Rigorous does not mean hard. Students' probes and assessments should be on their instructional level, meaning they have had direct exposure to the material they're being assessed on. If a student hasn't seen the content of their probes before administration, even if you/they learn something in the process of administration, it really has no value for the IEP goal. Probes and IEP goal data collection should be on the student's instructional level in all cases. So then, what does it mean to have rigorous data collection?

Rigorous data collection is about how the special educator modifies and adjusts the assessment based upon the changing instructional level of the student. Students do not often struggle with every goal the entire year. So, as students improve and as they approach mastery, educators have to be able to adjust and modify their probes so that the IEP team can accurately say whether the student has mastered the goal. This means special educators are providing different types of assessment to measure goals as students improve so that students with disabilities can effectively generalize the skills they've learned in different settings and formats. If a student can add two-digit numbers written vertically (as seen on their probes), but is completely lost when that equation is written horizontally, they haven't mastered the skill. If a student can do a task on paper, but not on a computer they haven't mastered the skill. Rigorous data collection isn't about making probes longer or more complex, it is about meeting students on their instructional level and making sure they have a holistic mastery of skills. Now special educators can very well write goals that are so specific that they don't account for the various formats in which students will be required to show competency such that if they don't need to modify the probes or assessments. It wouldn't be apparent that anything was lacking academically on the student's end if done this way because, well, they fulfilled the goal. However, this isn't rigor and it doesn't meet students where they are. If you take this bare minimum approach to progress monitoring and data collection students will always stay behind and at the mercy of how well their goals are written. Even poorly written goals can be tracked in a rigorous manner that pushes students forward.

Additionally, this speaks to why it is advantageous to write applicable IEP goals that state that assessments will be given on the student's instructional level rather than their specific grade level particularly if they have a diverse range of skills deficits. One example that is especially relevant for students is in reading fluency. Reading fluency deficits can and will include a variety of skills deficits like prosody, accuracy, and rate. If a 6th grade student who is four years behind in reading is given a reading fluency IEP goal that states the student will be given a 2nd grade level probe to track progress made at their end of the year IEP meeting, but over the summer they make growth in a summer reading program, when they return to school the following fall on the 3rd grade level the IEP goal will already be obsolete. If the special educator tracks that goal on the 2nd grade level the student will either show mastery too early and the future data collection will be redundant or the special educator may stop tracking that goal altogether after the student reaches that goal early in the year. Conversely, if the student's grade level is written in the goal, for far behind students like this one, the student will struggle so much with their probes that the data won't give an accurate measure of their progress and the probing won't produce any meaning practice (certain types of assessment like this can be a useful form a practice). What should happen is that the educator gives a probe on the student's instruction level (as the goal should say) and as that student's score shows consistent mastery on that grade level that student should be given the next level of difficulty. This is also a useful strategy for math calculation (another skill area that can be tiered up if the student improves).

Special educators have to remember teaching itself is about rigor just like any other type of training. When you go to a physical therapist or a trainer, they are going to increase the level of the exercises they prescribe until you get to some intended point of mastery. The same is true of educational training. Too often progress monitoring and data collection is viewed in terms of 18-36 weeks of packets with the same problems, in the same order, stated in the same way regardless of if the goal is mastered. Special educators have to think about data collection in terms of rigor in which probes can change shape, format, and language. Ultimately, this means every probe should be on the student's instructional level whatever that may be.

Collaborative Data Collection

As mentioned in previous chapters of your survival guide, special education is not a field in which one can achieve with an "I'm better than the rest" mindset. Special education is far too complex for any one educator to believe (errantly) that they can achieve and be the best of the best in their school and/or community on their own like some high-level content specialist general educators do. Special education is a team-oriented field. You can be the brightest star in the sky, but you still cannot do it alone. You need teamwork, trust, and collaboration. Therefore, your data collection also must incorporate collaboration.

In this technological age, in this age of ease and convenience, in this age of information and the need for accurate information there is no excuse for data collection to be privatized, yet this is what we see in a large portion of our special education departments. Data collection is viewed as exclusively for the case manager, and it isn't shared unless requested. Data is stored far too often in a physical space that is inconvenient to access. Data collection is poorly integrated (or not at all integrated) into the framework of instruction such that students aren't learning the skills they're being probed on unless they happen to be in the pacing guide. These attitudes toward data collection are not just inappropriate for students with disabilities, they are detrimental to them. Data collection has to be collaborative. If the case manager needs data or work samples, they need to have them digitally stored first and shared with any relevant service providers. Physical work samples are typically not relevant longer than a year. The practice must be to scan and upload probes and work samples on a regular basis so that those who need them can access them. After they're uploaded most physical work will be obsolete. Data collection must also be shared so that it is properly integrated into instruction. Over 30% of all IEP goals are academic. So, when we have (which often occurs) special educators who simply print probes at the end of the week, grade, and collect them without using that information to design instruction they're stripping away all manner of purpose, usefulness, and value out of the probe. These probes used to track IEP goals are not exams nor are they merely height charts for measuring how academically tall a student is getting. Probes are for modification, integration, and intervention. If the special educator is not taking the probes and reviewing them themselves or sharing them with relevant service providers to integrate that data into instruction, they are not using them appropriately.

I've worked as the only special educator in my entire building (and this is the only case in which you wouldn't share data collection with other service providers) and yet I still had to share data collaboratively with other stakeholders. Beyond the few times that a service provider actually needed my data collection, and often most importantly, I had to share the data with the student. The case manager/ student relationship is the most important relationship that you will have as a special educator. Still, your job as a special educator isn't to build that relationship around getting your student to like you, your job is to build that relationship around their growth and data. For their disability, for their deficits, students have to know what level they're on, how they're progressing, and where they're headed at all times. I cannot explain how many students with disabilities tell me that they don't know their reading level when I first met them when they're being served in reading (I'd like to say 99% of students because I can't say 100%). Some other things that they cannot usually tell me is what their skill deficits are in the subjects they're being served in and what their accommodations are. You have to discuss data with the student on an ongoing and regular basis. Data discussion is a key feature of collaborative data collection. This is especially true for goals that don't require direct probing. All of your data collection shouldn't require direct assessment, but rather observation is frequently applicable. If the special educator is tracking a behavior, but doesn't share that data with the student or other stakeholders the student is not going to improve as a result of that data collection. Without review and discussion there is no intervention response.

In all cases, data collection has to be collaborative. It cannot be treated in the same manner as the IEP itself that must be locked away for security purposes. It has to be actively and readily shared in a collaborative manner to promote necessary intervention and program integration. Every special educator must keep in mind the following: data collection must be accessible to service providers, data collection should be virtual (meaning sharable), it must be discussed on a regular basis, it must be used to guide instruction.

Flexible Data Collection

When it comes to being flexible with data collection, this happens to be where special educators give the most pushback for reasons you and I may not understand. Flexible data collection means adjusting your data collection strategy based upon the most useful and meaningful strategy available at the moment. I've seen so many special educators use the same ineffective worksheets and packets to probe every single student and goal for no reason other than it's familiar. Yet, what they have available to them are online platforms, digital tools, interactive forms and activities, and other more effective data collection measures. When presented with these tools they may respond with "It's too confusing. They're (students) not used to it.". Now, I'm not a psychologist (again special educators are not clinicians), but these special educators are projecting their insecurities about managing different programs onto their students to the students' detriment. When I taught elementary school (with students with disabilities with many processing and skill deficits) I had at least 2 different logins for each student for programs they needed to use to track their data and goals. Sure, it took about 10 minutes for some to log in the first time, but the second time it only took 5. By the next week, it took 2 minutes max for them to log in. Moreover, they actually enjoyed it. Where would those students be if I hadn't trusted them to learn something new for a short time?

Special educators have to be able to adapt to the most useful strategy in all things, but especially with data collection. They have to train their students to be flexible and to respond to change effectively. Even the most obstinate student, even students with autism who don't respond well to change can adapt when it is taught to them effectively (and most students will not have this issue). Special educators have to be flexible to incorporate the most effective measure and strategy available. Sometimes this even means doing something, which should be far easier than not, like taking evidence of student progress directly from their classwork instead of probing in some cases. If you aren't sure about what tool or strategy is more effective, have a discussion with another member of your department, but remember to be willing to make a change. Fear of change is the enemy of progress.

Data collection is a difficult thing to master, but it is also deceptively simple. You have to create a system and a routine that helps you get everything done in a timely, effective fashion. In special education we often talk about the first 30 days of the school year in which the special educator must assign caseloads, print IEPs, set up their classes, provide accommodations, make a calendar for upcoming IEP meetings, and create a routine with co-teachers. However, the second 30 days of the school year should be spent creating and mastering a data collection system that will allow you to collect your data easily throughout the year. This means printing out all the probes that you'll need right away or at least organizing them on a flash drive, setting up all of the virtual programs for your students, putting together your data collection binder or spreadsheet so that the data you collect is shareable, and otherwise planning ahead. Consequently, the special educator will be far less stressed out throughout the year. Furthermore, in the case that you find something that works better for you, you'll be prepared to adjust. There's no reason for special educators to struggle with data collection at the end of the year. The system should already be working for them.

Chapter 9: The Teaching of Reading

It's time to talk about the teaching of reading. This chapter will be important, but distinctly different from the other chapters of your survival guide because 1) This isn't a chapter about how to teach a reading class and 2) Teaching reading isn't particular to special education, it has to do with general pedagogy and not just special education. So, you may be asking yourself if we're not talking about how to teach reading, what are we going to be discussing? Rest assured you will be receiving some tips and strategies for teaching reading to students with disabilities in this chapter, but I will not be going in depth to discuss all of the various skills and tools a teacher needs to support reading instruction. That is a whole other very long book. I would actually suggest *Teaching Reading Sourcebook* by Honig et al. You also may be asking yourself if the teaching of reading is a general education skill that isn't specific to special education, why are we discussing it in a special education survival guide? Well, the answer to that question is a good segway into the rest of this chapter. Reading is the single most important skill for students to learn.

Millions of dollars have been spent on marketing campaigns aimed at getting students to read. The skill of reading isn't just important because reading makes you "smarter", reading is the key to accessing any and all types of knowledge. Whether you're in school and need to learn anything beyond basic math, science, social studies, or any core subject, reading is necessary to gain access to that information. If you want a professional job, if you want to be a chef, or if you just want to travel, reading and reading well is necessary to know what to do and how to do it. From the burning of books to the printing press, over the course of history reading and access to reading has been used as a means of both oppression and liberation. There is no more important skill that a student will ever learn in a K-12 education. Moreover, because the skill of reading is so important to all students it is especially critical for students with disabilities.

The reality is our modern classrooms, schools, and districts are full of students who are behind in reading because they didn't learn to read well the first time they were taught. Once they fall behind, they stay behind and fall further behind regardless of whether they have an IEP or not. In fact, it is a fairly well known anecdote that 3rd grade reading scores are used to predict the number of beds needed inside prisons. Although hard to believe it is true this indeed is a slippery slope. I cannot tell you how many students with disabilities that I've met, who have been added to my caseload that were 3+ years behind in reading fluency in elementary, middle, and high school. Beyond their disability and the relative difficulty that the disability creates in obtaining reading proficiency, these students with disabilities are often behind because they aren't given relevant specially designed reading instruction.

When it comes to all things IEP, students with disabilities are provided specially designed instruction as all aspects of their educational program must be specifically designed to address the needs of their educations and disabilities. Specially designed instruction is most obvious in self-contained classes where the student is being instructed based upon a modified curriculum. Every part of that instruction is clearly specially designed. It isn't as clear for students receiving special education services who are provided the general curriculum. This is true because the curriculum is the same for students without disabilities and the accommodations provided may be similar to things you might see in a general education classroom. Regardless of where you see it, specially designed instruction must be provided in all settings and cases. However, when it comes to the teaching of reading, students with disabilities are often being prescribed lessons, programs, and assignments that aren't specially designed and aren't relevant to their IEPs.

I've experienced situations where students who cannot read in elementary school are given highlighters as accommodations to illuminate words or lines of text that they cannot read independently in the first place. I've witnessed middle school students spend their entire class periods working on online grammar programs that teach identifying punctuation and parts of speech when they read 3-5 years behind in grade level reading proficiency. I've seen high school students struggle through oral reading activities until they give up or cause a behavior disturbance. Let me be clear this is unacceptable. Although accommodation is a general good, for the teaching of reading to students with disabilities the instruction must be relevant instruction on their instructional level. Many special educators make the excuse that "administration" told them that what they do in the reading class should "mirror" what is taking place in the general education class for students who receive the general curriculum. That is only true to the extent that you as the special educator are providing relevant specially designed instruction.

It is a different case when the student is only 1-2 years behind in reading fluency (sometimes that can be remedied by accommodations and goal setting), but when the student is 3/4/5 years behind in reading proficiency that student has to be provided reading instruction on his instructional level. This means that student is spending routine time in his classroom working on reading texts on his level and improving his reading fluency level. When I taught students with severe skill deficits like this, I would also hear all the time that "they" want us to do what the general education teachers are doing. They'd say that they want us to mirror instruction. Some days I would take their worksheet, lesson plan, or activity and say we'll look at it (maybe 10 minutes of my class maybe more) to show we've reflected something general education was doing, but often I would tell them no we're not working on that. If questioned, I would tell them that these students with disabilities according to their IEPs need a certain type of instruction and the amount of time it takes to teach this small aspect of the general curriculum cannot take precedence over the academic needs identified by their IEPs.

Now, everyone doesn't possess this same level of advocacy, but let's be clear, relevant instruction is not focusing on gerund phrases and past participles in a 5th grade small group reading class of students who are 4 years behind in reading fluency on average. Specially designed instruction is not just "mirroring" any and everything that a general education teacher does while providing accommodations (especially when the general education teacher would have provided the same accommodations anyway). Granted, high functioning students will see more of what general education teachers provide more often; instruction is differentiated. However, in all cases reading instruction has to be modified to the students with disabilities' needs. Students with disabilities must receive specially designed instruction in reading (like all subjects).

This chapter, again, is not about how to teach a reading class, but on the other hand it is. Special educators need to come to terms with the fact that students who function on the 3rd grade level in reading will require 3rd grade level reading practices to improve. They cannot focus every class period (which is happening to students with disabilities today) on gerund phrases, subjunctive mood, and other perfunctory skills in the general curriculum when reading fluency (as identified by their IEPs) – the ability to read and identify words with ease and fluidity – by far and away is the most important skill they will learn in elementary, middle, high school, and beyond. This is also true of reading comprehension which we haven't discussed much in this chapter because reading comprehension improves with reading fluency. Also reading comprehension is a skill that exists in the curriculum of every grade level while reading fluency is not taught directly in the curriculum beyond 3rd grade. It is therefore the responsibility of the special educator to teach that reading fluency when it is necessary. Additionally, special educators can make the mistake of focusing too much on reading comprehension for students who have no fluency by reading the texts they practice aloud to them or with them. If you read the texts to the student (even as an accommodation) the skill begins to change from reading comprehension to listening comprehension.

Now, you may be wondering what is the secret to effectively teaching reading and modifying instruction for students with disabilities (particularly those who lack reading fluency). I won't be telling you everything about how to teach reading in this chapter (I suggest you take an actual teaching of reading course or read a book on the subject, they are very beneficial), but I will provide you with some best practices that will lead you in the direction of improving student reading levels hand over fist. Oftentimes, no matter how well we understand the teaching of reading and how to provide this instruction, without these practices students will still struggle to show growth. These practices are most useful for students who are below or far below grade level fluency.

Teaching of Reading Best Practices

- Assess every student on your caseload's reading level if they are in elementary or middle school
- Assess every student on your caseload's reading level if they have reading services
- For students being served in reading, give them a reading level assessment at the beginning of the year and toward the end of the year (at least twice to measure growth)
- Identify the recommend usage time for any virtual reading program students use in the classroom (do not sit them on the same program all class period)
- Use a reading fluency assessment that has tiered vocabulary for grade level alignment
- Do not rely on universal screeners to assess your student's reading level (Do it yourself)
- If your student is more than 2 years behind in reading fluency and below the 8th grade level in reading

fluency give them an oral reading probe on their instructional reading level every week
- Provide reading fluency homework to students
- Give the students sight word and vocabulary activities
- If the student is not growing after 3 probes, provide an intervention
- Do choral reading and guided questioning
- If the student reads 120 wpm or more on their weekly reading fluency probe more than twice in a row, that is fluency, move them to the text with the next level of difficulty

I cannot tell you how many special educators I've seen kneecap their student's reading growth simply because they don't administer their own assessments, they don't reassess reading levels at the end of the year, they don't provide interventions and use the same level probe no matter how quickly the student reads. These practices may not seem very mind-blowing, because they're not, but they aren't that intuitive either. There are so many special educators that allow outside factors (like what gen ed is doing, what lesson plans need to look like, and what their department chair has already given them) dictate what best practices they actually implement in their classrooms and for their caseloads. It doesn't matter if the superintendent personally made a suggestion and spent 5 million dollars on a reading program that people say is the bee's knees, students with disabilities are in special education because they need specially designed instruction so special educators have to be strategic in providing individualized and evidence-based practices to maximize their students' growth.

Please, don't take anything shared in this chapter lightly. Reading is that important. Every year that I've taught I've met at least a few students who are years behind in reading proficiency who are also being provided or have been provided irrelevant instruction. If a special educator were to fail at every aspect of a student's education program one year, but managed to teach that student with a disability to read fluently they may have dramatically changed their life for the better. Special educators must teach students with disabilities to read.

Chapter 10: Your Philosophy

Congratulations you've made it to the final chapter of your survival guide! At this point, you should know much of every and anything you need to do to be successful in this field of special education. You know what attitudes you should have, what practices you should keep and avoid, and you know the importance of the work that you are going to be doing. You have a strong foundation and you can do this!

Now we really need to talk about one final thing that largely determines what of these practices you actually integrate into your work as a special educator. That thing is your teaching philosophy. Why do you do this work?

Every teacher has a different reason for teaching. Some do it because they like small children. Some teach because they like sharing knowledge. However, for the special education teacher their philosophy isn't just a reason or a rationale, it is highly impactful to their work outcomes. Special education isn't just about learning, teaching, liking kids, doing activities, field trips, college prep, or any of the other typical features of education. It is about advocacy, empowering parents, creating independence, leveraging strengths, removing obstacles, and opening pathways. A special educator whose teaching philosophy isn't intertwined with the student with a disability is either not going to be as effective as they should be in their role or not going to stay in that role very long. I recognize that for some teachers as soon as they step inside of a classroom for the first time it's a foot race to see how quickly they get an administrative position at the end of the building where all they have to do is make slides and tell other teachers what to do. That might work for some people, but for the special educator to do the work the way it needs to be done their teaching philosophy has to be in some way tied to the student with a disability.

When I did co-teaching, I always made it very clear that I was there for the student with a disability. As long as one teacher was supporting the student with a disability when they needed it, I was okay. Yet, if I was ever given the option to support a student with a disability in the classroom, regardless of the need, I made it known that I will always choose the student with a disability over a general education student every single time. I don't care if that student with a disability is the most unlikeable student to ever use a #2 pencil. I don't care if the general education student is the funniest, smartest student and even if they have a bigger concern. I will always address the student with a disability first. That is what special education is about; putting students with disabilities first. The reality is some students with disabilities in their lives will be forced to be independent before they're ready. Some will never be independent their entire lives. Some may have the option to be. The special educator can make a difference in those outcomes. Every action that a special educator takes in relation to a student with a disability must be in service of the future in which that student is the most joyful, the most prepared for life, and the most free. That is the thinking behind my classroom decisions.

This is what it means to survive and thrive in special education. Thriving in special education is about knowing what you need to do, having all of the tools you need, and being joyful in the work. Surviving is about overcoming the adversity related to education and special education, and making your mission about students with disabilities so that when you come into work you know why you're there and who you're there for.

What is your teaching philosophy for special education?

If you don't have one that is okay. You can make one or even change it. However, when you do make your teaching philosophy make it so you survive in the work, make it so you thrive in the work.

Selected Bibliography

All Star Staff. 2019. "A Short History of Special Education | All
    Education Schools." AllEducationSchools.com. March 8,
    2019. https://www.alleducationschools.com/blog/history-
    of-special-education/.

DeLussey, Stephanie. 2023. "The Power of Impact Statements in
    IEPs." The Intentional IEP. November 16, 2023.
    https://www.theintentionaliep.com/impact-statements/.

"ECTA Center: IDEA." n.d. Ectacenter.org.
    https://ectacenter.org/idea.asp.

"Eligibility Categories." n.d. Www.gadoe.org.
    https://www.gadoe.org/Curriculum-Instruction-and-
    Assessment/Special-Education-Services/Pages/Eligibility-
    Categories.aspx.

Haughey, Duncan. 2014. "A Brief History of SMART Goals."
    Project Smart. December 13, 2014.
    https://www.projectsmart.co.uk/smart-goals/brief-
    history-of-smart-goals.php.

"IRIS | Page 3: Transition Planning." n.d.
    Iris.peabody.vanderbilt.edu.
    https://iris.peabody.vanderbilt.edu/module/cou2/cresour
    ce/q1/p03/.

Karthik, Kumar. n.d. "What Are Considered Moderate to Severe
    Disabilities?" MedicineNet.

https://www.medicinenet.com/moderate_to_severe_disab
ilities/article.htm.

Kesherim, Ruben . 2023. "Behavior Intervention Plan: Definition
& Examples." Www.supportivecareaba.com. June 22,
2023. https://www.supportivecareaba.com/aba-
therapy/behavior-intervention-plan.

Morin, Amanda. n.d. "Reevaluations for Special Education."
Www.understood.org.
https://www.understood.org/en/articles/reevaluations-
for-special-education.

Parent to Parent of Georgia. 2019. "Special Education Law."
Parent to Parent of Georgia. May 10, 2019.
https://www.p2pga.org/roadmap/education/special-
education-
law/#:~:text=Family%20Educational%20Rights%20and
%20Privacy%20Act%20(FERPA).

"Special Factors." n.d. Family Network on Disabilities.
https://fndusa.org/special-education-downloadable-
resources/special-
factors/#:~:text=Special%20Factors%20in%20the%20IE
P%20Development&text=The%20special%20factors%20
are%20behavior.

U.S. Department of Education. 2020. "Free Appropriate Public
Education (FAPE)." Www2.Ed.gov. January 16, 2020.
https://www2.ed.gov/about/offices/list/ocr/frontpage/p
ro-students/issues/dis-issue03.html.

———. 2021. "Family Educational Rights and Privacy Act (FERPA)." *U.S. Department of Education*, August. http://www.ed.gov/policy/gen/guid/fpco/ferpa/index.html.

———. 2023. "Free Appropriate Public Education under Section 504." *Ed.gov*, July. http://www.ed.gov/about/offices/list/ocr/docs/edlite-FAPE504.html.

www.ingramcontent.com/pod-product-compliance
Lightning Source LLC
Chambersburg PA
CBHW062113080426
42734CB00012B/2842